SILKWORM REARING TECHNOLOGY
PRINCIPLES AND MANAGEMENT

By

Dr. Tribhuwan Singh
Scientist-C
Research Extension Centre
Central Silk Board, Ministry of Textiles
Govt. of India, Rampur Road
Una (Himachal Pradesh)

Dr. Pramod Kumar Singh
Scientist-D
Regional Sericultural Research Station
Central Silk Board, Ministry of Textiles
Govt. of India, Sahaspur
Dehradun (Uttrakhand)

and

Dr. Khursheed Ahmad Sahaf
Director
Central Sericultural Research & Training Institute
Central Silk Board, Ministry of Textiles
Govt. of India, Pampore
Jammu & Kashmir
(INDIA)

DPH

DISCOVERY PUBLISHING HOUSE PVT. LTD.
NEW DELHI-110 002

Published by:
Tilak Wasan

DISCOVERY PUBLISHING HOUSE PVT. LTD.
4383/4B, Ansari Road, Darya Ganj
New Delhi-110 002 (India)
Phone : +91-11-23279245, 43596064-65
Fax : +91-11-23253475
E-mail : discoverypublishinghouse@gmail.com
sales@discoverypublishinggroup.com

website : www.discoverypublishinggroup.com

First Edition: **2015**

ISBN: 978-93-5056-696-1

Silkworm Rearing Technology: ***Principles and Management***

Printed at:
Infinity Imaging Systems
Delhi

Preface

Sericulture is the science which deals with the production of silk by rearing of silkworm. Silk is called the 'queen of textiles' due to its glittering luster, softness, elegance, durability and tensile properties. Silk originating in spittle of an insect is a natural fibrous substance and is obtained from cocoons spun by larvae known as silkworm. The silk is preferred over all other types of fibers due to its remarkable properties like water absorbency, heat resistance, dyeing efficiency and luster. Silk perhaps is the only product next to gold in India, enjoying ever-growing domestic market and the love for owning the natural wonder fiber is persisting from centuries.

India has unique distinction of being only the country in the world to produce all the four commercial variety of silk – Mulberry, Tasar, Eri and Muga. As India encompasses with wide geographical and agro-climatic variations, mulberry sericulture is distributed in temperate, sub-tropical and tropical regions, while the major production comes from the tropics. Mulberry silkworm (*Bombyx mori* L.) is very delicate, highly sensitive to fluctuating environment and unable to survive extreme natural fluctuation in temperature and humidity because of their long years of domestication since more than 5000 years. Temperature, humidity, air circulation, gases, light and nutrition show a significant interaction in their effects on different developmental stages of silkworm affecting growth, production, productivity and quality of silk.

Different components such as mulberry cultivation for production of quality mulberry leaves as a source of feed for silkworm, method of silkworm rearing technology for healthy growth and development of larvae, silkworm egg production technology to maintain productivity and quality besides protection of silkworm and mulberry from pests and diseases to reduce crop losses, processing and reeling of cocoons etc., have been well defined. As a result, country experienced a quantum jump in silk production and India emerged as the second largest producer of silk in the world next only to China. In recent times, cocoon production has been considered as an important cash crop from the status of a very traditional and small subsidiary crop of marginal returns. Thanks are due to the pioneering efforts of Indian sericulture scientists to improve production and productivity per unit area. In fact, sericulture industry in India has been making steady and sustained progress through planned approaches. The current improvement in production, productivity and quality has made Indian sericulture highly attractive and remunerative to the farmers.

Among the various aspects of sericulture science, the one on '*silkworm rearing*' deals with the information required for planning the silkworm rearing for production of quality cocoons in higher quantity per unit area on scientific lines by adopting technological advancements achieved on the subject. Quality is the product of technology and inputs. Input refers to inter alia breed, quality of seed cocoons and harvestation of stable cocoon crop produced by adopting improved package of practices of silkworm rearing technology (higher survival rate, higher pupation rate, disease freeness, maintenance of optimum temperature, humidity, ventilation and light, infrastructure facilities, technical manpower availability etc.).

Silkworm rearing is labour intensive economic activity in which mulberry leaf is converted into silk cocoons by feeding silkworms on good quality mulberry leaves. Silkworm crop is harvested after short duration and guarantees periodic income to economically poor seri-farmers. Silkworm rearing is very important aspect of sericulture industry. Successful silkworm rearing depends on the perfect understanding of nutritional and environmental conditions required for different developmental stages of silkworm. Failure of silkworm crop is often attributed to non-adoption of recommended package of practices of silkworm rearing besides bad management.

Although, enough information is available elsewhere on rearing methodology but in-depth information on commercial silkworm rearing for production of quality cocoon/silk in Indian conditions has becomes essential. Also the information available in the books published in the past is outdated and no more in use. Therefore, it was thought desirable to publish a comprehensive book on '*Silkworm Rearing Technology – Principles and Management*'. The present publication is self-contained document. In this book theoretical as well as practical aspect of silkworm rearing has been explained lucidly. This book is designed to address wide range of readers, experts, university teachers, students, researchers, technologists, policy-makers and to fulfill the hopes and aspirations of all those engaged in sericulture in general and cocoon production in particular. It will serve as a very useful guide and will motivate and assist in the efforts to find solutions to the existing problems in order to increase production, productivity and quality of silk. This book has many unique features. It comprises chapters on various silkworm breeds and hybrids authorised for commercial rearing in different regions and seasons of the country; mulberry varieties authorised/released for cultivation at farmers level; disinfection of rearing establishments to maintain disease free environment at rearing places and to maintain hygiene; incubation of silkworm eggs for uniform hatching and healthy growth of larvae; package of practices for chawki and late age silkworm rearing to harvest quality cocoons; mounting and mounting methods, various types of mountages and their suitability to achieve sustained and quality cocoons with increase production and productivity besides technology of cocoon harvest, transport and marketing. The information furnished in this book will be of immense importance not only to Indian sericulture but also to South Asian and African countries and will find an application at all levels of sericulture.

To present the comprehensive and updated information in this book '*Silkworm Rearing Technology – Principles and Management*', we have drawn necessary information, photographs and scores from published books, documents, periodicals, journals, technical reports etc., and help taken from all of them is gratefully acknowledged.

It is with great pleasure, we wish to express our sincere thanks to all those we had interactions and enlightened discussions which stimulated and prompted us to take up this onerous task of compiling all the available information on mulberry silkworm rearing. We wish to place on records our profound thanks to all those friends and well wishers who have directly or indirectly helped in one way or the other and for the constant encouragement in bringing out this publication. A reliable guide and lovable compilation, this book is sure to appeal all those associated directly or indirectly with sericulture industry.

We profoundly thank Sri Tilak Wasan, Director and Publisher, Discovery Publishing House Pvt. Ltd., New Delhi whose interest and enthusiasm have brought out this book with an excellent presentation within a short period.

All-out efforts have been made to incorporate correct and authentic information in the present book. Nevertheless, we accept all the responsibility for any omission or deficiency that might have crept inadvertently, inspite of our best efforts and intensions, please brings out such errors to the notice of the authors and publishers. The views and suggestions from users of this book are welcome to improve upon future editions.

Authors

Contents

CHAPTER 1

Introduction

Sericulture in India is viable agro-based industry aptly matches with the socio-economic back-drop of the rural region of the country. Silk, the queen of fibres, is the fruitful culmination of the cumulative and concerted efforts of the multi-disciplinary functionaries like cocoon producers, egg producers and reelers, weavers etc. Indians are the largest consumers of silk, second largest producer of silk, largest importer of mulberry raw silk and producers of all four commercially exploited silk in the world *viz.*, Mulberry, Tasar, Eri and Muga and has been recording consistent growth in the quality, production and productivity. As India encompasses wide geographical and agro-climatic variations, mulberry sericulture is distributed in temperate, sub-tropical and tropical zones, while the major share comes from the tropical regions. Prior to independence, mulberry raw silk production was only 800 MT per year and sericulture was considered as a subsidiary occupation of the poor farmers. In fact, popularization of improved agronomical practices, release of improved mulberry varieties, evolution of productive silkworm breeds and hybrids coupled with crop protection measures and appropriate rearing and reeling technologies besides different package of practices developed for increasing production and productivity of cocoon/silk, changes the whole sericulture scenario in 1980s. The contribution of R&D resulted increase in cocoon production from 294 kg/ha/year in 1975-76 to about 772 kg/ha/year in 2011-12. Raw silk productivity increased from 20.34 kg/ha in 1975-76 to 93.00 kg/ha in 2011-12. The renditta, which is the most important parameter to judge the quality of silk, has come down from 14.5 kg in 1975-76 to 7.65 kg in 2011-12. The raw silk production has now reached to 18,272 MT from 2,541 MT in 1975-76 (Table 1.1). The cocoon yield/100 DFLs has increased from 21.52 kg in 1975-76 to 55.23 kg in 2010-11. The credit for these achievements goes equally to the present day sericulturists with a receptive mind, willing to readily take up the challenges for better quality and productivity on one hand and to the pioneering efforts of Indian sericulture scientists and extension personnel on the other, who are striving hard to develop suitable region and season specific technologies, and take them to the field. Today, Indian sericulture represents a picture of an established, flourishing and well organized industry spread all over the country, made a phenomenal progress in silk production and emerged as the second largest producer of silk in the world only after China.

Sericulture is an agro-based industry and here "we cannot apply yesterday's methods today and be in business tomorrow". Therefore, to keep pace with the brisk changes in the technology, sericulture community should know and adopt useful research findings developed from Research Institutes from time to time. The need for adoption of new technologies arises out of the fact that the conditions of the rural people in general and sericulture farmers in particular, have to be improved from the present state of affairs. There is a wide gap between the actual situation and the desirable situation thought to be. This gap has to be narrowed down by use of science and technology in their enterprises and bringing appropriate changes in their existing situations.

Table 1.1: Mulberry Sericulture in India

Year	Reeling Cocoon Production (MT)	Raw Silk Production (MT)	Renditta	Raw Silk Productivity / ha (kg.)	Cocoon Productivity / ha (kg.)	Cocoon Productivity / 100 DFLs (kg.)
1975-76	36739	2541	14.50	20.34	294.12	21.52
1985-86	76717	7029	10.90	32.27	352.40	29.18
1990-91	116663	11486	10.15	36.28	368.48	36.78
2000-01	124663	14432	8.64	66.84	577.35	39.17
2001-02	139616	15842	8.81	68.26	601.60	41.84
2002-03	128181	14617	8.77	75.17	659.15	43.90
2003-04	117471	13970	8.41	75.46	634.57	45.21
2004-05	120027	14620	8.21	85.02	698.00	46.79
2005-06	126261	15445	8.17	86.25	705.11	48.09
2006-07	135462	16525	8.20	86.12	705.92	47.70
2007-08	132038	16245	8.13	87.84	714.00	49.87
2008-09	124838	15610	8.00	87.72	701.56	51.78
2009-10	131661	16322	8.07	88.82	716.43	52.85
2010-11	130714	16360	7.99	90.20	767.49	55.23
2011-12	139871	18272	7.65	93.00	772.39	NA

MT: Metric Tonnes; NA not available.

Silkworm is one of the most important domesticated insect, which produces luxuriant silk thread in the form of cocoon by consuming mulberry leaves during larval developmental period. The growth and development of silkworm larvae is greatly influenced by microclimatic environmental conditions. The biological as well as cocoon related parameters are influenced by ambient temperature, rearing seasons, quality mulberry leaf and genetic constitution of silkworm breeds/hybrids. The seasonal differences in the environmental components considerably affect the genotypic expression in the form of phenotypic output such as cocoon weight, shell weight, shell ration, renditta, survival percentage, cocoon yield etc. Success of sericulture industry depends on several variables, but rearing technology and ambient environmental conditions during rearing are of particular importance. If the quality of egg is good, mulberry variety is excellent, and rearing practices adopted is perfect, one can harvest a successful crop and if it is inferior, the crop could be lost at any stage of the silkworm rearing depending on the magnitude of the defects. Quality is the product of technology and inputs. Input refers to silkworm breeds; quality of seed cocoons; rearing technology and management adopted; and their impact (survival rate, pupation rate, disease freeness, maintenance of optimum temperature, humidity, aeration and light, infrastructure facilities available, technical manpower availability, technology used etc).

The factors responsible for deterioration of quality of cocoons are poor quality of leaf, unhygienic conditions during silkworm rearing, non-maintenance of optimum micro-climatic conditions (temperature, humidity, photoperiod, ventilation) and lack of knowledge besides low-level technology adoption. To overcome all these problems, efforts are being focused for the improvement of quality by –

- Adoption of better management strategies for procurement of quality silkworm eggs from Government grainages/ Licensed Seed Producers (LSPs) only.
- Farmers should not prepare silkworm eggs by themselves for rearing.

- Adoption of recommended technology of disinfections of rearing establishments.
- Adoption of effective and efficient egg transportation technology from egg producing centres to chawki rearing centres.
- Adoption of improved incubation technology and maintenance of ambient environmental conditions as per recommendation.
- Introduction of season and region specific high productive silkworm breeds and hybrids as authorised and released by Central Silk Board for commercial rearing to ensure better production, productivity and profit.
- Adoption of improved package of practices of chawki and grown silkworm rearing and maintenance of optimum micro-environmental conditions in the rearing establishments.
- Introduction of eco-friendly custom designed equipments for silkworm rearing, mounting of spinning larvae and harvesting of cocoons.
- Adoptions of price fixation strategy for commercial cocoons especially in those areas where there is no cocoon market to ensure sale of cocoons within reasonable time at appropriate rate.
- ISO certification of silkworm chawki rearing centres for quality maintenance.

A number of reviews, handbooks and bulletins are available to describe rearing technology for mulberry silkworm to harvest quality cocoons on certain specific lines or as a part of book chapters (Ayuzawa *et al.* 1972; Krishnaswamy *et al.* 1973; Wu and Chen, 1992; Krishnaswamy, 1986, 1993; Ullal and Narasimhanna, 1994; Dandin *et al.* 2000; Kawakami, 1999, 2002). However, these are inadequate to reflect comprehensive and fool-proof scenario in order to enrich the knowledge of sericulture farmers, students, researches and scientists etc. Besides policy-makers to take appropriate decision and strategies for implementation to harvest better quality and higher quantity of cocoon. Further, several new technologies have been incorporated relatively recently and many of the old concepts have been changed. Therefore, it was thought desirable to publish a comprehensive book on '*Silkworm Rearing Technology – Principles and Management*'. The present publication is self-contained document. In this book theoretical as well as practical aspect of silkworm rearing has been explained lucidly.

This book on '*Silkworm Rearing Technology – Principles and Management*' is a compendium of existing relevant information on silkworm rearing encompassing new technologies developed relatively recently and updated. This book therefore, provides comprehensive details of mulberry silkworm rearing technology and their management written to cater to the specific needs of Indian States. This publication aims at serving the basic needs of sericulture farmers *i.e.*, production of healthy silkworm crop for harvesting better quality silk. This as a reference book will be of immense help to the students and teachers of sericulture; to the scientists working in labs and in the field; to the sericulture extension workers and for general academic/professional interest. Attempts have been made to –

- Discuss silkworm breeds and hybrids authorised by Central Silk Board for commercial rearing in different regions and seasons in Indian States, its systematic position, life cycle, external morphology and nature of classification, voltinogenesis besides improved mulberry varieties authorized and released for cultivation and utilisation during silkworm rearing to harvest stable cocoon crop with better quality.
- Discuss the disinfection and maintenance of hygiene, preparation of different types of disinfectant solution required for disinfection of rearing establishment, effectiveness of bed disinfectants etc., to contain occurrence of diseases during silkworm rearing to harvest stable cocoon crop.

- Discuss incubation techniques, maintenance of environmental conditions required during incubation, method of black boxing to obtain uniform hatching within short period with healthy larvae.
- Discuss package of practices of chawki and late age silkworm rearing technology, maintenance of optimum environmental conditions during rearing; mounting techniques, various types of mountages and their uses.
- Cocoon formation, its characteristics, harvest of cocoons, deflossing, transportation and marketing.

CHAPTER 2

Silkworm Breeds and Hybrids

The insect producing mulberry silk is domesticated variety of silkworm which is believed to have been derived from the wild variety known as *Bombyx mandarina* (Moore). Mulberry silkworm (*Bombyx mori)* belongs to the phylum – Arthropoda, order – Lepidoptera; class – Insecta and family – Bombycidae. It is under division Endopteregota and undergoes complete metamorphosis with egg, larva, pupa and adult (moth) in its life cycle.

Classification of Silkworm

Phylum	:	Arthropoda.
Class	:	Insecta.
Sub-class	:	Pterygota.
Division	:	Endopteregota.
Order	:	Lepidoptera.
Super family	:	Bombycoidia.
Family	:	Bombycidae.
Genus	:	*Bombyx.*
Species	:	*Mori* (Linnaeus).

Salient Features

Insecta

- Body is metamerically segmented and bilaterally symmetrical.
- Body is divided into three distinct regions *i.e.,* head, thorax and abdomen.
- Head bears one pair of antennae and usually one pair of compound eyes.
- Thorax consist of three segments, bears three pairs of jointed legs, usually with two pairs of wings which, may be sometimes one pair and rarely absent (louse).
- Insects are the only invertebrates that can fly.
- Abdomen is divided into 7-11 segments, which are without ambulatory appendages in the adult.
- Sexes are separate (diocious).
- Fertilization is usually internal.
- Insects are also known as hexapoda due to presence of six legs (3 pairs).

Lepidoptera

- Insects with two pairs of membranous wings.
- Body, wings and appendages covered with minute overlapping scales forming colored pattern.
- Metamorphosis complete.
- Fore wings always larger than hind wings.
- Larvae are typical caterpillars with biting mouthparts, three pairs of thoracic legs (true legs) and five pairs of abdominal legs (pseudo legs).
- Adult mouthpart is of sucking type, maxillae modified into coiled proboscis.

Bombycoidea

- Proboscis absent or rarely developed.
- Antennae pectinate.
- CU_2 absent from both the wings.
- Maxillary palpi and tymphanal organs absent.
- Chetosema absent.

Bombycidae

- No proboscis.
- Antennae pectinate in both the sexes.
- Larvae elongated with mediodorsal horn (caudal horn) on the eighth abdominal segment.
- Producing silk.

Species of Silkworms

The insects which are utilised for the production of commercial silk includes the following species –

1. Mulberry silkworm *(Bombyx mori* Linnaeus).
2. Japanese tasar silkworm *(Antheraea yamama* Guerin).
3. Chinese tasar silkworm *(Antheraea pernyi* Guerin*).*
4. Tasar silkworm *(Antheraea mylitta* Drury).
5. Muga silkworm *(Antheraea assama* Heifer).
6. Eri silkworm *(Phiiosamia cynthia ricini* Boisduval).

India is the only country in the world producing all the four commercially known variety of silk *i.e.,* mulberry silk (*Bombyx mori);* tasar silk *(Antheraea mylitta),* muga silk *(Antheraea assama)* and eri silk (*Phiiosamia cynthia ricini).*

Life Cycle and External Morphology of Silkworm

Among the caterpillars, which can produce silk, the mulberry silkworm (*Bombyx mori*) is the one that produce most beautiful product. Silkworm is a holometabolous insect and passes through a complete metamorphosis from egg to the adult stage. The two other stages between egg and adult are larva (caterpillar) and pupa (cocoon).

Egg

The silkworm eggs are tiny and measure approximately 1.0-1.3 mm in length and 0.9-1.2 mm in width. Eggs may be ovoid, flat, ellipsoid or oval with micropyle at the anterior pole and slightly off-centre. Mostly, the freshly laid eggs are pale yellow or dark yellow in colour. The colour of hibernating eggs laid by bivoltine or multivoltine breeds changes and becomes dark brown or purple.

Shape, Size and Color

Takami (1946) reported that eggs of the silkworm (*Bombyx mori*) belong to non-regulative type. It is short, spheroid, slightly attenuated at the anterior end where the micropyle is situated and laterally flattened. The shape of egg is entirely dependent on the shape of chorion, which is formed in maternal body. Hence, the egg shape is inherited pseudo-maternally. Though, the size and weight of eggs varies from breed to breed, voltinism to voltinism and even season to season but it is approximately 1.0-1.3 mm in length, 0.9-1.2 mm in width and 0.6 mm thick (Miya, 1984) having 0.5 mg weight and about 1.075 specific gravity. Eggs may be ovoid, flat, ellipsoid or oval with micropyle at the anterior pole and slightly off-centre. Average size of eggs of different types of breeds is presented in Table 2.1. Among the eggs of a moth, the ones which are being laid first are heavier than those laid later. The egg weight changes due to environmental conditions and even the eggs of same genotype have weight variations due to differences in the rearing conditions. The average major axis and minor axis of silkworm eggs are 1.22 ± 0.03 mm and 0.98 ± 0.02 mm respectively.

Table 2.1: Average Size of Eggs of Different Types of Breeds of Silkworm

S. No.	Types of Breeds	Length of Egg (mm)	Width of Egg (mm)
1.	Japanese	1.30	1.21
2.	Chinese	1.29	1.21
3.	European	1.43	1.27
4.	Indian (Mysore)	1.05	0.87

Except few exceptions (white and red eggs), the eggs (*Bombyx mori*) are usually brownish yellow in colour. Generally deep coloured eggs are common in Japanese breeds, while eggs of Chinese breeds are commonly light in colour. Usually, the chorion is colourless and semitransparent and hence the yolk colour is easily observable through shell in newly laid eggs. Yolk is normally light yellow in colour but in some genotypes, it is dark yellow. The colour of yolk is entirely dependent on the maternal genotype, having a close relation to the haemolymph colour and cocoon colour of the mother moth (Tazima, 1964).

The colour of egg is also due to the colour of serosal cells. The pigment present in serosal cells is attributed to one of the amino acids – tryptophane. The pigment is formed in a series of steps in a sequence: tryptophane ➔ oxytryptophane ➔ formylkynurenine ➔ kynurenine ➔ 3-hydroxykynurenine ➔ chromogen ➔ chrome (pigment). In this series of reaction, certain enzymes participate. The eggs in which pigment is not formed, indicates absence of enzymes resulting in white eggs. The eggs receive gluey substance of moth on the underside during deposition to adhere to the substratum/ egg card. The gluey substance is being secreted from the sebific gland or accessory gland, opening at the vestibulum.

Eggshell (Chorion)

A new generation begins at the moment of fertilization of an oocyte by an appropriate sperm. After fertilization, a series of well-defined structural and biochemical changes occurs within the oocyte leading to genesis of offspring (Margaritis, 1985). For these processes to occur successfully, the egg has to be enclosed in such an entity as to permit embryogenesis to proceed safely. The major role played in this direction is by an oocyte covering, which is commonly referred as eggshell. The physiological function of eggshell is –

- To allow and facilitate sperm penetration into the egg for fertilization which will lead to genesis of offspring.
- To protect oocyte from unfavorable environmental conditions such as extreme temperatures, high humidity, dryness (Yamashita and Hasegawa, 1985) and pathogenic attacks (Hinton, 1981).
- To ensure adequate oxygen supply for all bio-chemical reactions occurring within the developing embryos and at the same time getting rid off carbon-dioxide.
- To provide elasticity for easy oviposition and facilitate hatching at the end of embryogenesis.

The insect eggshell or chorion in mulberry silkworm can be discriminated into four spatially differentiated regions *i.e.*, the anterior pole region (which has the specialised area for sperm entry), the posterior pole region, the ventral and dorsal regions and lateral flat region (Kawaguchi *et al.* 1996). The eggshell is very complex, multilayered, multiregional, supra-molecular structure. There are three major layers in any insect shell: *(i)* the vitelline membrane, *(ii)* the endocrine and *(iii)* the exocrine. The exterior layer is thin with rough web-like sulci and stripes; the second layer is much thicker than exterior with a structure of stripes and granules, the inner layer is very thin with a construction of multipores. Eggshell is made mainly of chorionin, which is composed of scleroprotein and some sacchriode and lipoid. The major amino acids composed of scleroprotein are presented in Table 2.2. The eggshell is produced by mesoderm follicular epithelial cells, which are the parts of follicle. Each ovariole contains approximately 50-60 follicles at various stages of oogenesis. Eggshell formation is a gradual process involving certain cellular activities. Such activities have been recognised and analysed morphologically and bio-chemically in *Antheraea polyphemus* and *Bombyx mori.* *(See table on next page)*

Micropyle and Vitelline Membrane

The surface of micropyler region shows a petal like pattern, with the opening of micropyler canals at its centre. The micropyler canals are normally 3-4 in number but in some cases 6-8 canals have also been observed. Each micropyler canal can be divided into two parts – a tube penetrating the chorion and a protrusion connecting the tube to the vitelline membrane. The former is designated as 'ectomicropyle' and the latter 'endomicropyle'. In addition to micropyle, there are about 5000-10000 tiny pores around the egg surface. These pores permit air entry to meet the requirement of oxygen during embryonic development.

Table 2.2: Amino Acid Content in the Chorion of *Bombyx Mori Eggs*

Amino Acid	Outer Layer	Middle Layer	Inner Layer
Glycine	36.8	35.0	18.2
Alanine	8.5	3.1	8.3
Serine	3.2	4.5	6.7
Tyrosine	8.1	1.5	2.2
Valine	6.1	5.1	6.0
Asparagine	4.0	4.9	9.6
Gutamic acid	3.7	3.5	11.6
Threonine	3.3	2.0	5.1
Lysine	0.1	0.4	2.5
Phenylalanine	1.9	1.2	0.15
Isoleucine	3.3	2.1	3.8
Arginine	2.3	3.2	3.5
Leucine	6.4	1.4	7.0
Proline	4.3	2.3	10.1
Histidine	0.4	0.0	1.1
Methionine	0.0	0.4	1.1
Cysteine	5.8	29.6	0.5
Tryptophan	1.8	0.8	0.7

Beneath the chorion is very thin vitelline membrane enclosing the serosa and semi-liquid fluid (yolk), which fills the eggs. The vitelline membrane is secreted uniformly and its formation starts after the degeneration of nurse cells *i.e.*, at the time when oocyte occupies almost the entire egg chamber. The vitelline membrane is composed of an electron dense outer layer and an inner layer containing abundant irregularly shaped electron dense granules of various sizes.

Composition of Silkworm Eggs

The bio-chemical composition of silkworm eggs varies depending on the variety, season and environmental conditions. However, normal composition of eggs is presented below (Table 2.3).

Table 2.3: Bio-chemical Composition of Silkworm Eggs

S. No.	Component	Percent
1.	Protein	~ 10.00
2.	Lipid	~ 8.50
3.	Glycogen	2.00 ~ 5.00
4.	Chorion	14.00 ~ 18.00
5.	Water	63.00 ~ 65.00

Larva

Larva is popularly called silkworm caterpillar. It is the developmental stage of ingestion and nutrient accumulation to begin from newly hatched larva and end before spinning. Newly hatched silkworm larvae are black or dark brown in colour. It has a large head and body. The body is covered with bristles. There are four pairs of tubercles *i.e.*, sub-dorsal, supra-spiracular, infra spiracular, and basal tubercle, each of which carries three to six setae. Young larvae soon after hatching start feeding on mulberry leaves and grow. This period is called first instar. After three days, larvae stops feeding and after 20-30 hrs they under go ecdysis. The period of ecdysis is called the first moulting. After moulting, larvae starts feeding again, grow in size and weight and repeat the moulting process. In the common silkworm race, there are four moults and five larval instars. The duration of larval instars varies with the breed, temperature, humidity etc. Silkworms from first to third instars are referred as young (chawki) age silkworms and fourth and fifth instars as advanced (late) age silkworms. The fifth larval stage is the longest larval stage and shows maximum consumption of leaf. The growth rate during this stage is also extremely high. At the end of 5th stage, larvae stops feeding and start spinning from spinneret. In appearance, the larvae at this stage become lustrous and translucent. This stage is known as mature silkworms. From this stage onwards, the larvae spin cocoon and once the cocoon formation is over, the larvae moults inside and transforms itself into pupae. This is known as pupation.

The body of silkworm is divisible into head, thorax and abdomen. The thorax is composed of three segments and abdomen eleventh segments. Inter-segmental membranes join the successive segments. The head is composed of six segments, which are fused together. The second, fourth, fifth and sixth segments carry appendages, which are modified in to antennae, mandibles, maxillae and labium respectively. There are six pairs of ocelli or larval eyes, which are located behind and a little above the base of antennae. The antenna is five segmented and is used as sensory organ. The mandibles are well developed and powerful and are adopted for mastication. Maxillae consist of cardo, strips, maxillary lobe and maxillary palpi. Maxillary lobe and maxillary palpi discriminate the taste of food. The thorax, which is consists of three segments are called pre, meso and meta-thorax. Each of the three thoracic segments has one pair of legs. Each leg is composed of three jointed segments, which carries sharp distal claws. These legs are referred as true legs. The claws help in holding the mulberry leaves while the larvae are feeding on it. The abdomen consists of eleven body segments, wherein last three segments *i.e.,* 9th, 10th and 11th are fused together to form 9th segment, anal plate and the caudal legs. Thus, only nine segments can be distinguished in the abdomen. Each 3rd, 4th, 5th, 6th and 9th abdominal segment bears a pair of abdominal legs. These legs are fleshy, unjointed muscular protuberances and are known as pseudo-legs. Eighth abdominal segment on the dorsal side carries caudal horn. The abdominal legs at the extremity form a sort of disc with a series of inwardly curved hooks, which are arranged in semicircle and helps in crawling of the larvae. The abdominal segments on the ventral side of 8th and 9th segments carries sexual markings, which develops distinctly in 4th and 5th instars. In the female, the sexual markings appear as a pair of milky white spots, one each on the right and left side in 8th and 9th abdominal segments. These spots are known as Ishiwata's glands. The anterior pair situated in the 8th abdominal segment is known as Ishiwata's fore gland and the posterior pair in 9th segment is referred as Ishiwata's hind glands. When the female larvae pupate and transformed in to an adult, the anterior Ishiwata gland becomes a pair of bursacopulatrix, recepticulum seminis and its duct while the posterior Ishiwata glands are modified to form the posterior part of oviduct and accessory gland. The reproductive gland in the male silkworm appears as a small milky white protuberance at the centre of the ventral side between 8th and 9th abdominal segments. The gland is known as Herold's gland. When the larva transforms in to an adult, the Herold's gland develops in to seminal vesicle and ejaculatory duct. The male and female can be distinguished based on these glands during early 5th instar larvae. There are nine pairs of spiracles placed laterally on either side of the body. They are found on the first thoracic segment and from 1st to 8th abdominal segments. The spiracles are the part of respiratory system. Between the first and second thoracic segments, there is a pair of rudimentary spiracle. The size of the spiracles varies from breed to breed, individual to individual and from segment to segment. The spiracles on the 8th abdominal segment are the largest whereas those on the 2nd, 3rd and 4th are the smallest.

Pupa

The pupal stage is generally called resting or inactive stage in the life cycle of the silkworm, when it is incapable of feeding. This is a transitional stage during which definite changes take place. The mature silkworm larva passes through a pre-pupal stage before transforming in to pupa. During pre-pupal stage the dissolution of the larval organs takes place and this is followed by formation of adult organs during the pupal stage. At the pupal stage, a pair of large compound eyes, a pair of large antennae, fore and hind wings and legs is prominent and it is much easier to differentiate male and female in the pupal stage than in the larval stage. Soon after pupation the pupa is white in colour and soft and gradually turns brown or dark brown and the pupal cuticle becomes harder. The prominent pupal parts visible at this stage are a pair of large compound eyes, a pair of large antennae, fore and hind wings and the legs. While ten segments in the pupal body are visible from the ventral side but only 9 such segments can be seen from the dorsal side. The sex markings are more visible and very easy to differentiate male and female at this stage than at the larval stage. The female pupa on the ventral side has a fine longitudinal line joining the 8th and 9th abdominal segment, while such a marking is absent in the case of male, which has a small opening in the 9th segment. Usually female is bigger and heavier than the male. Various tissues and organs present in the larva undergo histolysis in pupal stage and tissues and organs of the adult are in the process of histogenesis in this stage. There is no ocelli, abdominal appendages, silk glands, moulting glands etc. The cuticle of a freshly formed pupa is very soft and pale yellow in colour and gradually becomes darker.

Adult

The adult moth emerging from the pupa is called silk moth, which is incapable to fly because of its domestication for more than five thousand years. It does not feed during its adult life. The body of the moth is composed of three distinct segments *viz;* head, thorax and abdomen. The antennae are prominent, bipectinate and serrate. Two compound eyes are situated on either side of the head below the base of the antennae. In normal silk moths, compound eyes are usually black in colour due to tryptophane metabolites. The ocelli are absent. The mouthparts are located between the two compound eyes. The thorax consists of three segments namely prothorax, mesothorax and metathorax. The mesothorax is the largest and is pentagonal. All the segments are covered with hard chitinous scelrites. Each of the thoracic segments bears a pair of legs. Each of the thoracic leg is composed of five segments. The meso and meta-thorax bear two pairs of wings – the fore wings and hind wings. The fore wings are larger, triangular in shape and are attached to the mesothorax. The fore wings overlap the hind wings when the moth is in the resting position. The hind wings are smaller and are attached to the metathorax. The surfaces of wings are covered with fine scales. Thorax bears a pair of spiracles. Morphologically, male and female moths can easily be distinguished in the adult stage. In male silk moth while eight abdominal segments are visible, female have only seven such segments. There are six pairs of spiracles situated laterally on either side of the body. Female is less active than male and has smaller antennae, large blunt and fatter abdomen. At the caudal end, the male moth has a pair of hooks 'harps', while the female has knob like projections covered with sensory hairs.

Body Temperature

As silkworm is poikilothermic, their body temperature fluctuates with changes in external environmental conditions. With the progress of development, the body temperature increases. Temperature is higher during the peak period of feeding and decreases thereafter. The factors affecting the body temperature of silkworm is ambient temperature, humidity, ventilation, supply of mulberry leaves and accumulation of waste materials in the rearing bed and population of density of larvae per unit area. Body temperature of pupa is low compared to 5th instar larvae but as soon as pupa metamorphoses into adult, the body temperature again increases. However, temperature of 24-28^{0}C and humidity of 75-85 per cent is ideal for all activity of silkworm. Higher or lower the temperature than the optimum affects crop stability in various ways.

Nature of Classification

Silkworms are classified in different ways. For example, the classification may be based on distribution, number of generations in a year (voltinism) or even the number of larval moults. Silkworms are also being classified according to the pattern of larval markings, body colour of larva and cocoon besides colour of eggs etc.

1. Classification based on Distribution

Broadly the silkworms are classified into two categories, *viz; (i)* temperate and *(ii)* tropical races. Based on geographical distribution, the silkworm's races are grouped into Japanese races, Chinese races, European races and South East Asian races.

(i) *Japanese Races:* Japanese races are univoltine and bivoltine having robust larvae and spin peanut shaped cocoons. These races can withstand bad quality leaf but are weak against high temperature. Cocoon filament is thick. Average cocoon weight is 2.3 gm; shell weight 0.55 gm, SR 24 per cent, and filament length 800-1500 meters and raw silk yield is 19 per cent.

(ii) *Chinese Races:* Chinese races are uni, bi and even multivoltine. Larval growth is quick. Larvae are usually plain and robust. It can withstand high temperature but are weak against high humidity, as well as low temperature. Shape of cocoon is elliptical or spherical in many races but some are spindle in shape also. Average bivoltine cocoon weight is 2-2.5 gm, shell weight 0.44-0.55 gm, SR 22 per cent with 16 per cent raw silk yield. Polyvoltine cocoon weighs 1.1-1.2 gm, shell weight 0.15-0.16 gm, SR 14 per cent with raw silk yield of 10-11 per cent. The cocoons are white, golden yellow, green or even pink in colour. The fibers are thin and their reeling is good.

(iii) *European Races:* European races are only univoltine. Larvae show light normal markings. Races are weak against high temperature and high humidity. Cocoons are large with mild constriction. Average cocoon weight is 2.0-2.4 gm, shell weight 0.46-0.61 gm, SR 23-25 per cent, filament length 1700 meter and raw silk yield 20 per cent. Generally the eggs, larvae and cocoons are larger than those of Japanese and Chinese races. Larval period is longer. Cocoons are white or buff coloured and fiber is longer with good reeling.

(iv) *South East Asian Races:* Usually multivoltine, hardy and have tremendous ability to survive and reproduce under fluctuating climate. Economic characters are poor. Cocoon shape in most cases is spindle. Cocoon weight is 0.9 gm, shell weight 0.1 gm, Shell Ratio 12 per cent, filament length 350 meter and raw silk yield is 6 per cent.

2. Classification Based on Moulting

During larval period at certain interval silkworms stops feeding, become inactive and shed their skin. This process is called moulting and the classification can be based on number of moults. These are –

(i) *Trimoulters:* Primitive type and is usually noticed in wild silkworm exhibited by three moults, short larval duration, small body and cocoon and fine silk filament.

(ii) *Tetra moulters:* Almost all present commercial silkworm races are tetramoulters, characterized by four moults with normal larval duration. They are reared for commercial exploitation.

(iii) *Pentamoulters:* These races are characterized by five moults, longer larval duration and large size filament. Occasionally few trimoulters or pentamoulters also appear in tetramoulting races. The dominance relationship is –

Tri > Tetra > Penta

Moreover, these moulters are under the control of M^3 allele series. These alleles are M^3, +M and M^5. Besides ecdysone hormone secreted by prothoracic gland also plays important role in determination of moulting.

M^3 allele ⟶ Brain ⇒ Prothoracic gland ⇒ Ecdysone ⇒ Moulting

3. Classification Based on Cocoon Color

Various varieties of silkworms are known producing different colours of cocoons such as white, yellow, golden yellow, green, greenish yellow, pink etc. These are broadly classified into white and coloured. The white ones are of two types – *(i)* inferior white and *(ii)* superior white. Among the white cocoons some are pure white, while others are dirty white. Coloured cocoons are of different type's *viz;* yellow, buff, straw, green, and golden yellow and so on.

Two main pigments are responsible for these colours namely, *(i)* carotenoids and *(ii)* flavonoids. Carotenoids are responsible for yellow and pink colour of cocoons. Carotenoids found in cocoon shell of silkworms are B-carotene, neo B-carotene, lutein, tetraxanthin, violaxanthin and sarcinaxanthin. As all these carotenoids are being reported present in mulberry leaf and hence it is being assumed that the pigment found in cocoon-shell might have derived from the mulberry leaves. Flavonoids are responsible for green and light green colour of the cocoon. The pigment 'flavone' is abundantly contained in mulberry leaves.

Yellow cocoon races have permeability only for carotenoids or its derivatives while greenish colour cocoon races have permeability only for flavonoids. But in white cocoon races, the intestinal wall is impermeable to all kinds of pigments. The genes which controls the permeability are –

- *Y gene*: Colour pigment (carotenoids and flavonoids) passes to haemolymph from intestinal mucosa (alimentary canal).
- *I gene:* Colour pigments are not allowed to pass to haemolymph. Haemolymph is colourless and hence the cocoons produced are white.
- *Y gene (silk gland cells)*: It allows carotenoid to pass to silk gland cells and hence yellow cocoons are produced.
- *Ga, Gb and Gc gene (silk gland cells)*: It allows flavonoids to pass to silk gland cells and hence light green or greenish colour cocoons are produced.

4. Classification Based on Rearing Period

Based on rearing period silkworms are classified into spring, summer and autumn races. The summer-autumn is further classified as summer, early autumn, late autumn and very late autumn silkworms.

5. Classification Based on Larval Markings

According to larval markings, silkworms are classified into two categories: *(i)* plain and *(ii)* marked. Three pairs of spots on the body represent normal marked silkworm larvae. These spots are located on the 2nd thoracic (mesothorax) segment (eye spot), 2nd abdominal segment (crescent or lunules) and 5th abdominal segment (star spots). Besides these, the other types of larval markings are stripes, dark colour, zebra bands, brown spots, quail marks, multistar, multilunar etc.

6. *Classification Based on Voltinism*

Voltinism is defined as a number of broods or generation in a year produced under natural conditions. Though genes located at different loci control the phenomenon of voltinism, but it is also under the control of temperature, photoperiod, humidity and nutrition. India has the unique distinction of being the only country in the world producing all the four commercial known varieties of silk. On the basis of voltinism, these silkworm races are classified as univoltine, bivoltine and multivoltine producing respectively one, two and many generations in a year. Different types of voltinism exhibited by silkworms are presented in Table 2.4.

Table 2.4: Types of Voltinism in Silkworm

Common Name	Family	Scientific Name	Voltinism
1. Mulberry silkworm	Bombycidae	*Bombyx mori*	Uni, Bi and Multivoltine
2. Tasar silkworm			
(*a*) Tropical	Saturniidae	*Antheraea mylitta*	Uni, Bi and Multivoltine
(*b*) Temperate	Saturniidae	*Antheraea proylei*	Bivoltine
3. Muga silkworm	Saturniidae	*Antheraea assama*	Multivoltine
4. Eri silkworm			
(*a*) Domesticated	Saturniidae	*Philosamia ricini*	Multivoltine
(*b*) Wild	Saturniidae	*Philosamia cynthia*	Uni and Bi

Mulberry silkworm (*Bombyx mori*) generally produces two types of eggs. These are hibernating and non-hibernating. In hibernating eggs, the embryo enters diapause after partial development and hatches out during the following spring while in non-hibernating eggs; the embryo develops without any interruption and hatches out in about 10 days. Univoltine lay only hibernating eggs, which are, also called Kurodane eggs while multivoltine lay only non-hibernating eggs, which are known as Nemadane eggs. The behaviour of bivoltine eggs are intermediate which lay non-hibernating eggs during first generation and hibernating eggs in the next generation which hatches out in the following spring and thus producing only two generations in a year.

Voltinogenesis and Silkworm Races

Though the status question of origin of different voltinic forms in silkworm has attracted many investigators but still no concrete information is available on the line. Prof. Yasikada, an eminent scientist of Tokyo university Japan who collected some 250 original silkworm races from different parts of world including univoltine, bivoltine and multivoltine stated the origin as –

Univoltine → Bivoltine → Multivoltine

The study was primarily based on acid phosphotase and esterase in haemolymph and epidermis. He found in total 15 types of phosphotase and esterases. Of these he noticed five types of phosphotase (A, B, C, D and O) and four types of esterase (A, B, C and O) in haemolymph and 6 types of esterases (A, B, C, AB, AC and O) in epidermis. He found all these fifteen types only in Chinese bivoltine races. Other silkworm races lacked one or the other esterases. Genetical theories also explain that ancient and wild type varieties would preserve most divergent genes in their genotypes. As the seasonal, environmental besides location affect the life strategies of living organism, univoltine races through mutational changes might have lost one or more genes corresponding to the missing esterases. Accordingly, Prof. Yasikada stated that univoltine silkworm is the earliest race originated about 5000 years ago in North China. This original race moved towards South China and got converted into bivoltine some 4000 years ago. When these voltinic forms moved to middle China (tropical zone) got converted into polyvoltine.

Famous Chinese sericulture scientist Prof. Tang Wai Leo of South China Agricultural University, Ghonzhou expressed different view on voltinogenesis. His explanation is based taking environmental conditions into consideration. According to him North China was a part of tropical and sub-tropical region. Due to drastic environmental changes, the tropical hot weather became cool and North China became temperate zone. Tropical weather started shifting towards south. Polyvoltine races also moved to South China but the indigenous polyvoltine in North China must have converted to bivoltine and stayed there. But continuous cooling of north ultimately compelled these bivoltine to change into univoltine to continue in the same region. The bivoltine, which were not able to survive there, were shifted to mid-China, while polyvoltine have been further pushed to South. According to him as univoltine races passed through divergent environmental conditions, has compelled them to develop divergent genes in their bodies to synthesize fifteen phosphotase and esterase. Thus the finding what was stated by Japanese scientist was advocated as correct but the explanation put-forth was contradicted. Hence, according to Prof. Leo, the original direction suggested by Prof. Yasikada was proved reverse.

Polyvoltine → Bivoltine → Univoltine

Indigenous Indian Silkworm Races

(a) *Barapolu:* It was the only univoltine silkworm race indigenous to India (Bengal). The larvae spin flossy cocoons of greenish white or pure white colour. One end pointed and compact cocoon, has short filament length. The race has now degenerated.

(b) *Chotopolu:* It was a univoltine race of Bengal. Larvae spin characteristically small, flossy, white or yellow cocoons. The race has now degenerated.

(c) *Pure Mysore:* Indigenous multivoltine race very popular in south India. Low productive race characterized by greenish yellow spindle shaped cocoons. It is suitable for subsistence farming conditions, fluctuating temperature and poor hygienic conditions. Produces soft and flossy cocoons (floss% 18-22%). Larval period is quite long (27-

28 days). Very poor post cocoon quality parameters with high renditta (11-12). It is said to have originated in China and brought to India in 1795.

(d) *Sarupat:* Multivoltine race reared in North Eastern part of India (Assam). Plain larvae spin small, flossy, light creamy white spindle cocoons.

(e) *Moria:* Multivoltine race of North Eastern India. The plain larvae build flossy and creamy white spindle cocoons. The cocoons are very small with only 15 kg yield/100 Dfls. It is not a very good combiner with existing races and hence not in use.

(f) *Kashmiri Race:* It is now extinct, which once produced famous Kashmiri silk. This race was univoltine, yielding yellow elongated oval cocoons.

(g) *Nistari:* Multivoltine race introduced in India in the year 1780-81 from China. The larvae of this race are small and spin soft and flossy golden yellow spindle cocoons. The race is very popular with the sericulturist of West Bengal. It is resistant to high temperature and high humidity. The yield/100 Dfls is low which, ranges from 15-22 kg only. It is very good combiner with many evolved multivoltine and bivoltine breeds.

Authorised Silkworm Hybrids and Mulberry Varieties

Both multivoltine and bivoltine silkworm hybrids authorised for commercial use is presented in Table 2.5 (Dandin *et al.* 2005). Table 2.5 also shows the seasons and regions of the country, where these authorised hybrids are to be reared by the sericulturists.

Mulberry is the sole food plant of silkworm. There was the need to develop high yielding mulberry varieties with excellent nutritive value for harvestation of stable cocoon crop with higher productivity. Therefore, effort was made and Indian scientists were able to evolve/develop varieties with high biomass and yield potential. The mulberry varieties cultivated/evolved over the years in India and released/authorised by Central Silk Board for commercial exploitation in Table 2.6.

Table 2.5: Mulberry Silkworm Hybrids for Different States and Seasons Authorised by the Central Silk Board (Approved by the Mulberry Silkworm Race Authorisation Committee) for Commercial Rearing

States/Regions/Zones	Combinations	Hybrids	Season	Date of Authorisation
1	2	3	4	5
Andhra Pradesh	Multi x Biv	P2D1 x NB18	Winter	31/07/1995
West Bengal	Multi x Biv Biv x Biv	MY1 x NB18 P2D1 x NB18 N x (NB18 x P5) SH6 x KA CA2 x NB4D2	Spring/Autumn Spring Autumn Spring/Autumn and Winter Spring/Winter	31/07/1995
Assam/Bihar/Orissa/ Madhya Pradesh	Multi x Biv Biv x Biv	MY1 x NB18 P2D1 x NB18 N x (NB18 x P5) PM x NB18 SH6 x KA CA2 x NB4D2 NB18 x P5	Spring/Autumn Spring Summer/Autumn Summer Spring/Autumn/ Winter Spring Winter	31/07/1995
Jammu and Kashmir	Biv x Biv	YS3 x SF19 SH6 x KA SH6 x NB4D2 CA2 x NB4D2	Spring Spring Spring Spring/Autumn/ Early Winter	31/07/1995

Contd...

1	2	3	4	5
		PAM101 x NB4D2 CC1 x NB4D2 PAM111 x SF19	Autumn/Early Winter Autumn/Early Winter Autumn/Early Winter	
Uttar Pradesh	Multi x Biv Biv x Biv	P2D1 x NB18 RD1 x NB18 YS3 x SF19 SH6 x KA SH6 x NB4D2 CA2 x NB4D2 PAM101 x NB4D2 CC1 x NB4D2 PAM111 x SF19	Summer/Early Autumn Summer/Early Autumn Spring Spring Spring Spring/Autumn/ Early Winter/ Autumn/Early Winter	31/07/1995
Rainfed Areas/Irrigated Areas South India Temperate/Sub-Tropical Zones	Multi x Biv Biv x Biv	BL23 x NB4D2 BL24 x NB4D2 CSR2 x CSR4 CSR2 x CSR5	Spring/Autumn Spring/Autumn Spring/Autumn Spring/Autumn	08/05/1997

Contd…

1	2	3	4	5
Temperate/Tropical Zones	Biv x Biv	CSR12 x CSR6 CSR18 x CSR19 CSR16 x CSR17 CSR3 x CSR6 KSO1 x SP2	Spring /Autumn Autumn Spring/Autumn Spring/Autumn Spring	04/05/99
North Zone (J and K and Uttaranchal)	Biv x Biv.	APS 5 x APs4 (HEMAVATHY)	Spring/Autumn	27/02/2002
South Zone	Multi x Biv	APM 1 x APS8 (SWARNANDHRA)	Spring/Autumn	
East Zone/South Zone	Multi x Biv	BL43 x NB4D2 (KAPILA)	Spring/Autumn	15/09/2005
South Zone and North Zone (Jammu and Kashmir)	Biv x Biv	(CSR6xCSR26) x (CSR2xCSR27) (Double Hybrid)	Spring/Autumn	15/09/2005
South Zone	Biv x Biv	CSR48 x CSR5 (Special breed for thin denier and long filament)	Spring/Autumn	15/09/2005
North Zone (Jammu and Kashmir, Himachal Pradesh and Uttaranchal)	Biv x Biv	Dun6 x Dun22	Spring/Autumn	15/09/2005

Contd...

1	2	3	4	5
South Zone	Biv x Biv	CSR2A x CSR4A (For rearing on semi-synthetic artificial diet at chawki stage)	Spring/Autumn	15/09/2005
South, East and North-East Zones	Multi x Biv	BL67 x CSR19 (CAUVERY)	Spring, Summer, Autumn and Winter/ late-autumn	15/09/2005
South Zone	Multi x Biv	PM x CSR2 (KOLAR GOLD)	Spring, Summer, Autumn and Winter/ late-autumn	15/09/2005
West Bengal	Multi x Biv	N x YB	Spring, Summer, Autumn and Winter/ late-autumn	15/09/2005
South Zone	Multi x Multi	BL67A x CSR101A (CAUVERY-A) (For rearing on semi-synthetic artificial diet at chawki stage)	Spring, Summer, Autumn and Winter/ late-autumn	15/09/2005
South Zone (in rain-fed Areas) West Bengal	Multi x Multi	BL24 x C. Nichi (VARUNA) N x M12(W)	Spring, Summer, Autumn and Winter/ late-autumn Dry summer (April-May) Wet summer (June-September)	15/09/2005

Contd...

1	2	3	4	5
Himachal Pradesh, Karnataka, West Bengal (Hills) and Assam	Biv x Biv	Dun17 x Dun18	Favourable seasons	16/04/2010
Andhra Pradesh, Tamil Nadu, West Bengal (Hills), Assam and Kashmir Valley	Biv x Biv	GEN3 x GEN2	Favourable seasons	16/04/2010
Uttarakhand, Himachal Pradesh, Uttar Pradesh, South Zones, Orissa, West Bengal (Hills), Assam and Mizoram	Biv x Biv	CSR 46 x CSR47	Favourable seasons	16/04/2010
Karnataka, Andhra Pradesh, Tamil Nadu (Hills), West Bengal (Hills), Assam, Mizoram and Kashmir Valley	Biv x Biv	SLD4 x SLD8	Favourable seasons	16/04/2010
Tamil Nadu (Hills) and Jammu Region	Biv x Biv	APS 45 x APS12	Favourable seasons	16/04/2010
Andhra Pradesh, Tamil Nadu (Hills) and West Bengal (Hills)	Biv x Biv	APS105 x APS126	Favourable seasons	16/04/2010
Karnataka, Himachal Prades and Jammu Region	Biv x Biv	KSO1x NP4	Favourable seasons	16/04/2010
Assam and Jammu Region	Biv x Biv	NK2 x NP4	Favourable seasons	16/04/2010
Uttar Pradesh, South Zones (Plains),West Bengal (Plains), Assam, Jharkhand and Manipur	Multi x Biv	PM x CSR2(SL)	Spring/Autumn	16/04/2010

Contd…

1	2	3	4	5
Karnataka, Andhra Pradesh, West Bengal (Plains), Tamil Nadu (Plains) and Jharkhand	Multi x Biv	Mcon-1 x Bcon-4	Spring / Autumn	16/04/2010
West Bengal (Plains), Orissa, Jharkhand and Assam	Multi x Biv	Mcon-4 x Bcon-4	Spring/Autumn	16/04/2010
Uttar Pradesh, Karnataka, West Bengal and Jharkhand	Multi x Biv	APM3 x APS12	Spring/Autumn	16/04/2010
Uttar Pradesh, Karnataka, Andhra Pradesh, Tamil Nadu and West Bengal Plains	Multi x Biv	APM2 x APDR105	Spring / Autumn	16/04/2010
Karnataka, West Bengal Plains and Jharkhand	Multi x Biv	APDR15 x APDR115	Spring / Autumn	16/04/2010
Uttar Pradesh, Karnataka, Andhra Pradesh, Tamil Nadu (Plains), West Bengal, Orissa and Assam	Multi x Biv	MH1 x CSR2	Spring / Autumn	16/04/2010
South Zones and West Bengal	Multi x Multi	Mcon-1x Mcon-4	Summer	16/04/2010
Andhra Pradesh, Tamil Nadu (Plains) and West Bengal	Multi x Multi	N x Mcon-4	Summer	16/04/2010
West Bengal	Multi x Multi	PM x C110	Summer	16/04/2010

Table 2.6: Mulberry Varieties Authorised by Central Silk Board for Commercial Use

Variety	Regions/Zones	Cultural Conditions	Date of Authorisation
V1	Karnataka, Andhra Pradesh, Tamil Nadu, Maharashtra and Kerala	Irrigated	25-10-2010
Anantha	Karnataka, Andhra Pradesh, Tamil Nadu, Maharashtra and Kerala	Irrigated	25-10-2010
Vishala	All sericultural regions in India	Irrigated	25-10-2010
S-1635	Karnataka, Andhra Pradesh, Tamil Nadu, Maharashtra, West Bengal, Uttar Pradesh, Bihar, Assam and other states in central India	Irrigated	29-12-2000
DD	Karnataka, Andhra Pradesh, Tamil Nadu, Maharashtra and Kerala	Irrigated	29-12-2000
S-36	Karnataka, Andhra Pradesh, Tamil Nadu, Maharashtra and Kerala	Irrigated	29-12-2000
S1	West Bengal, Uttar Pradesh, Bihar, Assam and Central India	Irrigated, Rainfed	29-12-2000
S-799	All sericultural regions in India	Irrigated	29-12-2000
S-13	Red soils of Karnataka, Andhra Pradesh and Tamil Nadu	Rainfed	29-12-2000
S-34	Black soils of Karnataka, Andhra Pradesh and Tamil Nadu	Rainfed	29-12-2000
BC-259	Hilly Eastern areas of India	Rainfed	29-12-2000
S-146	Central India, Doon Valley, Himachal Pradesh and Hilly Eastern areas of India	Rainfed	29-12-2000
Tr-10	Central India, West-North Jammu, Doon valley, Himachal Pradesh and hilly Eastern areas of India	Rainfed	29-12-2000
Chak Majra	Western North, Jammu and Himachal Pradesh (Sub-temperate)	Rainfed	29-12-2000
Chinese White	Western North, Jammu and western Himachal Pradesh (Temperate)	Rainfed	29-12-2000

The average leaf yield under rainfed conditions, which was approximately 4 MT only annually in 1950s, has increased to 18 MT in 1995. Similarly, under irrigated conditions, the leaf yield have shown tremendous increase from merely 15 MT to 45 MT. Relatively recently evolved mulberry variety V1 (Victory-1) is producing approximately 60-65 MT leaf yield annually under irrigated conditions. Most of the varieties cultivated in India, a major silk producing country in the tropical climatic regions shows high rate of growth, good response to pruning and producing more biomass.

Other than the mulberry varieties authorised by Central Silk Board for commercial use, there are few more mulberry varieties which are released based on their performance in the field (Table 2.7)

Table 2.7: Mulberry Varieties Released for Commercial Use

Variety	Breeder	Recommended for the Climate	Potential Yield / ha/ yr (MT)
K2	CSR and TI Mysore	Tropical	30.0
S-797	CSR and TI Berhampore	Tropical humid	25.0
C-776	CSR and TI Berhampore	Tropical humid	29.6
C-763	CSR and TI Berhampore	Tropical humid	32.0
S-30	CSR and TI Mysore	Tropical	41.3
S-41	CSR and TI Mysore	Tropical	34.0
S-54	CSR and TI Mysore	Tropical	40-50
RFS-135	CSR and TI Mysore	Tropical	40-50
MR-2	CSR and TI Mysore	Tropical	25.0
S-14	CSR and TI Mysore	Tropical	16.0
Gosheoerami	CSR and TI Pampore	Temperate	15.2

CHAPTER 3

Disinfection and Hygiene

The silkworm is affected by a large number of diseases caused by virus, bacteria, fungi and protozoa. These diseases are known to occur in almost all Sericultural regions of the world. The adverse environmental factors like temperature, humidity and poor quality of mulberry leaves reduces the tolerance of the host to the pathogens and hence increases susceptibility to infections. Disinfections and hygiene forms an integral part of healthy and successful silkworm rearing.. Crop losses due to incidence of diseases are one of the major problems encountered by sericulturists in India. The incidence of silkworm diseases and crop losses is greatly influenced by rearing practices, frequency of cropping; conditions of rearing houses, general hygiene and environmental conditions favourable for pathogen build up and spread (Pallavi and Kamble, 1997). Many pathogens, especially fungal and bacterial spores are light and can be drifted easily by air current, leading to spread of the disease. They have also the ability to remain alive in the environments for longer periods.

Silkworm eggs arriving in the rearing establishments from different sericulture regions of the country can form a continuous source of pathogen entry into the rearing units. Processing of batches continuously without providing sufficient time gap, leads to inadequate disinfection and thereby favours pathogen build up in the rearing establishments/ regions. Some of the facts about silkworm diseases are –

- All the infectious diseases of silkworms are caused by pathogens.
- The adverse environmental factor like temperature, humidity and feeding poor quality of mulberry leaf reduces the tolerance level of host to the pathogens and hence increases susceptibility to infections.
- The diseases of silkworms are highly contagious and spread very fast.
- There is no silkworm breed/hybrid, which is completely resistant to all the diseases.
- The silkworm pathogens survive longer in the rearing environment and remain infective.
- The diseases have atypical and typical morphological symptoms.

The disinfection can be defined as destruction of disease causing germs. It is the total destruction of diseases caused by pathogens. There is no curative method for any of the silkworm diseases and hence they can best be prevented rather than cured. This can be achieved by adoption of proper and effective methods of disinfection before and after every silkworm crop and or rearing operations. Therefore, to prevent crop losses due to diseases, disinfection is inevitable. Avoiding the spread of silkworm diseases is as much important as checking the spread of diseases in silkworm rearing. Continuous rearing without sufficient gap between the two batches does not provide opportunity for regular disinfection and therefore resulting in buildup of pathogens in the rearing establishments. Silkworm egg is the basic material determining success or failure of a cocoon crop and therefore adopting proper disinfection and hygienic method in preparation of silkworm seed is the foremost step towards raising a healthy silkworm crop.

Since, the species of microorganisms vary and situation in which they may occur differ greatly, no one or two methods are generally applicable. Each situation is a problem in itself and the methods employed depend on the knowledge, ingenuity and purposes of the operator. There are four main reasons for killing, removing or inhibiting microorganisms to maintain hygienic conditions. They are –

1. To prevent infection to man, his animals and plants.
2. To prevent spoilage of food and other commodities.
3. To prevent interference by contaminating microorganisms in various industrial processes that depends on pure culture.
4. To prevent contamination of materials used in pure culture work in laboratories (diagnostics, research, industry etc.).

Common methods of killing or removing microorganisms are –

- Destruction by heat (boiler, oven etc.), chemical agents (disinfectants), radiation (X-ray, ultraviolet rays etc.), mechanical agents (crushing, shattering by ultrasonic vibration) etc.
- Removal (especially bacteria) by filtration, high seed centrifugation etc.
- Inhibition by low temperatures (refrigeration, dry ice), desiccation (drying process), high osmotic pressures (lymph, brines etc.), chemicals and drugs etc.

Selection of Disinfectants

Several disinfectants are available in the market but only few are widely used. The disinfectants available in the market can be grouped as –

- Halogens (Chlorine, Iodine etc.).
- Heavy metals ($HgCl_2$, Mercurochrome, Metaphen, Protargol, etc.).
- Phenol compounds (Lysol, Creosols etc.).
- Alcohols (Ethyl and Isopropyl).

- Formaldehydes (strong reducing agent which inactivates even enzymes).
- Ethylene oxide (Carboxide, Cryocide etc.).

Qualities of an Ideal Disinfectant

Ideal disinfectant is selected taking into consideration of various factors. The ideal disinfectant must posses the following qualities –

- Highly effective against a wide variety of microorganisms in concentration as low as to be economical for use as well as harmless to human beings, domestic animals and non-toxic to plants.
- Non-injurious and non-staining to materials like fabrics, furniture or metal wares and non-offensive to odour or taste.
- As specific as possible for microorganisms.
- Does not damage the building, materials, appliances and equipments.
- A good surface tension reducer (have good wetting and penetrating properties).
- Stable in storage.
- Readily available in market and less expensive.
- Easily applied under household or other practical conditions of use.
- Completely microbicidal within a few minutes or an hour at the most and not inducing macrobiotics, leading to a false sense of security.
- Non-corrosive.

But, no single disinfectants have all these ideal properties. Some agents may be ideal under some conditions but not under others, *e.g.*, Cresol may be ideal for floors or sanitary purposes but harmful to infants.

Conditions Necessary for Effective Disinfections

It is established that disinfectants respond better under some specific conditions whereby disinfection becomes perfect and effective, such as –

- *Hydration*: Considerable quantity of water is required to facilitate the action of disinfectants, *e.g.*, dehydrated protein to coagulate is difficult since it will turn brown or char. Moreover, resistance of bacterial endospore to heat is probably caused in part by their extremely dehydrated conditions.
- *Time*: No disinfectant, as ordinarily used, acts instantly. Sufficient time for contact must be allowed for whatever chemical and physical reactions to occur. The time required will depend on the nature of the disinfectant, concentration, pH and temperature, nature of target organism and existence of the bacterial population of cells having varying susceptibilities to the disinfectant.
- *Temperature*: With respect to the microbicidal action of heat, temperature is inversely related to time. In case of chemical microbicides, as a rule, the warmer the disinfectant, the more effective is its action. Higher temperatures generally reduce the surface tension, increase acidity, decrease viscosity and diminish adsorption.
- *Concentration*: Effectiveness of a disinfectant is generally related to concentration exponentially, but not linearly. For example, doubling a 0.5 per cent concentration of phenol in aqueous solution does not merely double the killing rate. Doubling the concentration again may increase the effect by only a negligible amount. There is clearly an optimum concentration of phenol at about 1 per cent. Thus, a concentration of a disinfectant beyond a certain point accomplishes increasingly less and is wasteful.
- *pH*: An important factor in detergency is pH which is a measure of acidity or alkalinity. As the pH of the solution increases *i.e.*, becomes more alkaline, the efficiency of the product increases. There are limits to this, as too high pH will frequently result in deleterious effects on the surface being cleaned or disinfected. In general, a pH not higher than 10.5 is recommended. As a general rule, the lethal or toxic action of harmful agents involving

physical and chemical actions is increased by increased concentration of 'H' or 'OH' – ions.

- *Osmotic Pressure*: Fluids of high osmotic pressure (*e.g.*, food preserving syrups and brines) tend to dehydrate the cell contents and so increase resistance of microbial cells to heat and chemical disinfectants.
- *Surface Tension*: Surface tension is of basic importance in disinfection. There are two aspects of this factor, adsorption of surface disinfectants or interfering substances on the surface of the cells and the effect of disinfectants on the wetting and spreading properties of the solution. Both affect contact between disinfectants and microorganisms.
- *Materials Required for Disinfections:* Disinfectants, detergents, sprayer, buckets, jars, weighing scales (balance), gas masks, slaked lime, hand gloves and muslin clothes are required during disinfection.

Method of Disinfections

Disinfection methods are classified broadly of two types; *(i)* physical and *(ii)* chemical.

(i) Physical Methods (Burning, Burying and Exposure to Sunlight)

The physical method includes the use of physical agents such as ultraviolet radiation, flame, dry heat and streams etc. In sericulture, exposing the rearing equipments to bright sunlight for 8-10 hrs is a very economical method of disinfection under Indian conditions. Heat is the major destroyer. Dry heat destroys the microorganism by oxidation and is non-corrosive. Dry heat requires longer exposure time and or higher temperature. Use of boiling water is another effective method. The maximum temperature of 100^{0}C can be obtained and exposure of 10-30 minutes is found effective. Moreover, it is cumbersome and somewhat non-reliable method. However, best results can be achieved by a combination of both physical and chemical methods.

(ii) Chemical Methods

Chemical means of disinfection involves only those chemicals which have germicidal activity against targeted microbes. The use of chemical for disinfection achieved momentum since 1867, when Lister stated that phenol (carbolic acid) would kill microorganism. From then onwards, various chemicals have been tested for their germicidal activities and few of them are found effective in sericulture also. The most commonly used disinfectant in sericulture is formalin, bleaching powder, slaked lime, chlorine dioxide (sanitech/serichlor) and ashtra.

(a) *Formalin*: It is the most commonly used disinfectants in all sericultural countries. Formalin is aqueous solution of formaldehyde. It is commercially available in the form of 36-40 per cent formaldehyde. The specific gravity is 1.081 in 36 per cent and 1.087 in 40 per cent formalin. The molecular formula of formalin is CH_2O. The disinfecting action of formalin is due to reducing process of formaldehyde *i.e.* HCOH + O = HCOOH. Formaldehyde takes oxygen out of the germ cells leading to death of the germs. A mixture of 2 per cent formalin + 0.5 per cent slaked lime is very effective solution that can be used for disinfection purpose. Formaldehyde upon storage polymerizes into trioxymetylene, which is ineffective as spray and therefore storage of formaldehyde for long time is not advisable. The action of formalin takes place under wet conditions and therefore, the surface of equipments and walls should be drenched with the solution. The action of formalin is faster and more pronounced at temperature above 25^{0}C and humidity > 70 per cent. The action is greatly reduced at temperature below 20^{0}C. This mixture is more effective only if rearing houses/rooms/buildings could be closed to near airtight conditions. In India, more than 90 per cent of the rearing buildings are not suitable for disinfection with formalin as they are open type dwelling houses. However, formalin is also reported to be a carcinogen and therefore use of it as far as possible should be avoided.

(b) *Bleaching Powder*: Bleaching powder is also called chlorinated lime. It is white amorphous powder with a characteristic of pungent odour of chlorine. The efficacy of bleaching powder is very much dependent on the level of active chlorine in the compound (Balavenkatsubbaiah *et al.* 1994). For effective disinfection, a high-grade bleaching powder with active chlorine content of 30 per cent and above must be used. Bleaching powder when comes in contact with water produces weak acid (HCl) and releases nascent oxygen which has strong oxidizing action against germ cells. It should be stored in sealed bags, away from moisture and light to avoid degradation which rendered it ineffective. Freshly prepared solution of bleaching powder gives the best results. A 2 per cent bleaching powder in 0.3 per cent slaked lime is used for disinfection as spray. The action of bleaching powder is optimal under wet conditions and therefore, surface of appliances, equipments and walls of rearing rooms should be drenched with this solution.

(c) *Slaked Lime (Calcium Hydroxide)*: It is very cheap but effective and used as bed disinfectant besides drying agent in sericulture. It is not only environment and user friendly but also easily available. Lime is available in many forms in nature *viz*; calcite, calcium carbonate ($CaCO_3$, calcium hydroxide [$Ca(OH)_2$, calcium oxide (CaO), lime stone etc. Among the variety of lime, it is active lime which is required in sericulture. It absorbs moisture and can be used to regulate bed humidity and maintain hygiene in rearing buildings. It has strong antiviral action. Application of lime dust alone or in combination with bleaching powder in and around rearing houses and premises improves hygiene in the environment. It is prepared from burnt lime stone or shells by sprinkling water followed by pulverizing and sieving. Lime stone or $CaCO_3$ is burnt to produce quick lime (CaO) which when hydrated forms slaked lime (Calcium hydroxide) [$Ca(OH)_2$] which is used as disinfectant in sericulture.

(d) *Paraformaldehyde*: It is white crystalline substance with a strong odour of formalin formed by polymerization of formaldehyde. It is effective for fumigation purpose and is an ingredient of certain bed disinfectants. On heating, it sublimates and releases formaldehyde gas which inactivates the pathogens in wet condition and therefore the humidity of the room should be simultaneously increased to maintain the optimum level of requirement for rearing.

(e) *Chlorine Dioxide:* Chlorine dioxide (ClO_2) is marketed in different names such as sanitech, serichlor etc. It is an ideal disinfectant suitable for all types of rearing buildings. In combination with slaked lime, it is effective against all silkworm pathogens. It is a strong oxidizing agent, 2.5 times stronger than chlorine and two times stronger than sodium hypo-chloride and 50 times effective than bleaching powder. It is effective at broader ranges of pH and less reactive with organic compounds. It is least corrosive, non-hazardous and safe for use and user friendly. Chlorine dioxide (Sanitech) 500 ppm in 0.5 per cent slaked lime may be used for disinfection. It is stable and may be activated at the time of its use. It is recommended by Central Sericultural Research and Training Institute, Mysore and marketed by M/s Lakshmi Industries, Indore. Sanitech/Serichlor have many advantages (Rajan and Himantharaj, 2005) over other disinfectants *viz;*

- It is stable product containing precursor of chlorine dioxide which is released only on activation.
- Unlike chlorine, it does not dissociate or react with water but remains soluble in water like oxygen and exists as a gas in solution.
- The disinfectant at recommended concentration is least corrosive and possess tolerable odour.
- As it is contact disinfectant, it is effective in all types of rearing houses.
- Unlike ozone, it is also known to provide residual protection.

(f) *Asthra*: Multipurpose, broad spectrum room disinfectant recommended by Central Sericultural Research and Training Institute, Mysore and marketed by M/s Seri-Gro Products, Bangalore. For preparation of disinfectant solution, 50 gm of Asthra powder is added in 100 liters of clean water. The powder is mixed thoroughly in water and left for two hours. Spray Asthra solution two times per crop in rearing houses (1st spray after completion of rearing and 2nd spray 3 days before brushing date. 140 ml of Astra solution is required per square foot floor area of rearing house. Bleaching powder or other room disinfectants are not required is Asthra disinfectant solution is used for disinfection purpose. Rearing equipments are also disinfected with this solution.

Quantity Requirement of Disinfectants

Quantity requirement of disinfectant is estimated based on the surface area of the rearing building or trays to be disinfected. The quantity requirement may be estimated as –

(a) *Room*: (Total area in square meter)

Area of roof and floor	:	L × B × 2
Area of two opposite walls	:	L × B × 2
Area of two other side walls	:	L × B × 2
(b) *Rearing Trays:* (wooden/plastic)	:	L × B × 2 × Number of trays
(c) *Bamboo Trays*	:	$\Pi r^2 x$ 2 × Number of trays

The disinfectant solution should be prepared @ one liter per 2.5 square meters of area to be disinfected.

$$\text{Solution required in liters} = \frac{\text{Total area in square meters}}{2.5}$$

Preparation of Disinfectant Solutions

Disinfectant solution should be prepared a fresh before use.

(i) *2 per cent Formalin Solution:* Commercial formalin contains 36 per cent formaldehyde. This is diluted to prepare 2 per cent solution of formalin as follows:

$$\frac{\text{Concentration of available formalin} - \text{Concentration of formalin required}}{\text{Concentration of required formalin}} = \text{Parts of water to be added in one part of formalin}$$

i.e. $\frac{36 - 2}{2} = 17$ parts of water

or $N1V1 = N2V2$ or $V1 = \frac{N2V2}{N1}$ *i.e.* $V1 = \frac{2\text{x}100\ (\text{ml})}{36} = 5.55$

100.00 – 5.55 = 94.45 ml water; Ratio = 94.45: 5.55 = 17: 1

Where

N1 = Given strength of solution.

N2 = Desired strength of solution.

V1 = Volume of stock chemical required.

V2 = Desired volume of solution to be prepared.

Practically, for all disinfection purposes, one part of formalin can be mixed with 17 parts of water to prepare 2 per cent formalin solution (Table 3.1) from commercially available formalin (36%). Kumar *et al.* (2013) developed a software (seri-tool) with which if given strength and required strength of formalin solution is computed, it calculates the ratio of water and formalin for desired strength of solution.

Table 3.1: Preparation of 2 Per cent Formalin Solution of Different Quantities from 36 Per cent Stock Solution of Formalin

S. No.	Total Volume of Solution Required (liter)	Quantity of Formalin Required	Water to be Added (liter)	Ratio of Formalin: Water
1.	1.00	56 ml	0.944	1: 17
2.	5.00	280 ml	4.720	1: 17
3.	10.00	560 ml	9.440	1: 17
4.	15.00	840 ml	14.160	1: 17
5.	20.00	1.120 liter	18.880	1: 17
6.	25.00	1.400 liter	23.600	1: 17
7.	30.00	1.680 liter	28.320	1: 17
8.	35.00	1.960 liter	33.040	1: 17
9.	50.00	2.800 liter	47.200	1: 17
10.	75.00	4.200 liter	70.800	1: 17
11.	100.00	5.600 liter	94.400	1: 17

If commercial formalin contains 36 per cent formaldehyde, ratio of formalin and water in preparation of solution of different concentration of formalin will be as follows (Table 3.2).

Table 3.2: Preparation of Different Concentrations of Formalin

S. No.	Concentration of Formalin Required (%)	Concentration of Available Formalin (%)	Ratio of Water: Formalin
1.	1	36	35.00 1
2.	2	36	17.00: 1
3.	3	36	11.00: 1
4.	4	36	8.00: 1
5.	5	36	6.20: 1
6.	6	36	5.00: 1
7.	7	36	4.10: 1
8.	8	36	3.50: 1
9.	9	36	3.00: 1
10.	10	36	2.60: 1

(ii) *Formalin 2 per cent + 0.5 per cent Slaked Lime Mixture:* After preparation of 2 per cent formalin solution, slaked lime is added to it @ 5 gm in one liter of formalin solution. Slaked lime is prepared by sprinkling water on burnt limestone and pulverizes it into fine powder of 200-250 mesh size. The quantity required for disinfection may be calculated adopting the following procedure (example) –

Length of floor (L) = 20'
Breadth of floor (B) = 15'
Floor area for disinfection = L × B = 20' × 15' = 300 square feet or 28 m^2

The disinfectant required for disinfection of rearing house is @ 2 liter/square meter floor area or 185 ml/sq. feet floor area. Therefore, disinfection solution required = Total area × @ 2 liter/sq. meter or 28 m^2 × 2 = 56 liter.

Disinfection for outside the rearing house and appliances is to be added in this quantity. Additional disinfectant required for appliances is estimated to be 25 per cent of the solution required for floor area *i.e.* 56 × 25 per cent = 14 liters.

Additional disinfectant required for outside the rearing house is estimated to be 10 per cent of the solution required for floor area *i.e.* 56 × 10 per cent = 5.6 liters. Hence, total quantity of disinfectant required = 56 + 14 + 5.6 = 75.6 or 75 liters (Table 3.1).

(iii) 5 per cent Bleaching Powder Solution (Stable 30% chlorine): Solution of 5 per cent bleaching powder is prepared by dissolving 50 gm of the chemical in one liter of water (ratio; 1: 20). The mixture is agitated well. It is filtered through a layer of muslin cloth and the clear solution is used for spraying/disinfection. A ready reckonor for preparation of 5 per cent bleaching powder solution of different volumes is presented in Table 3.3.

Table 3.3: Preparation of Different Quantities of 5 Per cent Bleaching Powder Solution

S. No.	Total Volume of Solution Required (liter)	Bleaching Powder Required (gm)	Water to be Added (liter)	Ratio of Bleaching Powder: Water
1.	1.00	50	1.00	1: 20
2.	5.00	250	5.00	1: 20
3.	10.00	500	10.00	1: 20
4.	15.00	750	15.00	1: 20
5.	20.00	1000	20.00	1: 20
6.	25.00	1250	25.00	1: 20
7.	30.00	1500	30.00	1: 20
8.	35.00	1750	35.00	1: 20
9.	50.00	2500	50.00	1: 20
10.	100.00	5000	100.00	1: 20

The ratio of powder and water to be mixed for preparation of different concentrations of bleaching powder solution is presented in Table 3.4.

Table 3.4: Requirement of Bleaching Powder for Preparation of Different Concentration of Solution

S. No.	Concentration of Solution Required (%)	Quantity of Water (liter)	Quantity of Powder (gm)	Ratio of Bleaching Powder: Water
1.	1.00	1.00	10.00	1: 100
2.	2.00	1.00	20.00	1: 50
3.	3.00	1.00	30.00	1: 33
4.	4.00	1.00	40.00	1:25
5.	5.00	1.00	50.00	1:20
6.	6.00	1.00	60.00	1:17
7.	7.00	1.00	70.00	1: 14
8.	8.00	1.00	80.00	1: 13
9.	9.00	1.00	90.00	1: 11
10.	10.00	1.00	100.00	1: 10

$$\text{Quantity of chemical required} = \frac{\text{\% of solution to be} \times \text{prepared} \quad \text{quantity of solution required}}{100}$$

Example: (*a*) 2% of 1 liter solution $= \dfrac{2\% \times 1000\ (\text{ml})}{100} = 20$ gm

(*b*) 5% of 1 liter solution $= \dfrac{5\% \times 1000\ (\text{ml})}{100} = 50$ gm

(*c*) 2% of 75 liter solution $= \dfrac{2 \times 75{,}000\ \text{ml}}{100} = 1500$ gm or 1.5 kg.

(*iv*) *Bleaching Powder - Slaked Lime Mixture*: 2 per cent bleaching powder in 0.3 per cent slaked lime solution is used at the entrance and rearing building surroundings to maintain proper hygiene. For the purpose high-grade bleaching powder is mixed with finely powdered 200-250 mesh size slaked lime as presented in Table 3.5.

Table 3.5: Preparation of Different Volumes of 2 Per cent Bleaching Powder in 0.3 Per cent Slaked Lime Solution (Rajan and Himantharaj, 2005)

Total Quantity of Disinfectant (liter)	Bleaching Powder (kg)	Slaked Lime (kg)	Water (liter)
1.0	0.020	0.003	1.000
2.0	0.040	0.006	2.000
3.0	0.060	0.009	3.000
4.0	0.080	0.012	4.00
5.0	0.100	0.015	5.00
10.0	0.200	0.030	10.00

(v) *Slaked Lime Powder*: Burnt rock lime (limestone) or shell lime is procured, water is sprinkled and it is allowed to become powder. This is further pulverized, sieved and made into the form of fine powder, which can be readily used. Application of lime dust in and around rearing building and premises improves hygiene in the environment.

(vi) *Chlorine Dioxide (Sanitech 20,000 ppm stable)*: It is powerful, users' friendly, non-hazardous, safe and effective disinfectant for silkworm rearing house and equipments. Unlike formalin, it is non-carcinogenic. It is capable of successfully destroying microbial and all silkworm pathogens. Sanitech is 2.5 times more potent than chlorine and 50 times more effective than any hypochlorite like bleaching powder. Demands no airtight conditions of rearing houses for its action. There is no limitation of temperature and humidity for its action. Sanitech do not have corroding action on metallic items and rearing equipments at the recommended concentration. It remains in association with water as oxygen does in water. Sanitech is effective on a broad pH range (pH: 5-9). It does not give pungent smell or suffocation. As it is a contact disinfectant, it is effective in all types of rearing houses. Chlorine Dioxide (500 ppm) in 0.5 per cent slaked lime can be prepared as –

- *Solution A*: Add 50 gm of activator crystal to 500 ml Sanitech (ClO_2) solution to activate chlorine dioxide, stir and allow 10 minutes for complete dissolution of crystals. Colour changes to light yellow. Add the prepared 500 ml yellow solution to 19 liters of water to get 19.5 liter of solution.
- *Solution B*: Dissolve 100 gm of slaked lime powder in 500 ml water in another clean container and allow for some time to settle down.

Mix solution A and B to obtain a total of 20 liters of disinfectants. One liter of Sanitech makes 40 liters of disinfectants. For disinfection of one square meter of area, two liter of Sanitech solution is required. To prepare 2.5 per cent Chlorine Dioxide in 0.5 per cent slaked lime solution of different quantities, the requirement will be as detailed in Table 3.6.

Table 3.6: Preparation of 2.5 Per cent Chlorine Dioxide in 0.5 Per cent Slaked Lime Solution

S. No.	Volume of Solution Required (liter)	Quantity of Sanitech Required (liter)	Water to be Added (liter)	Activator Crystal Required (gm)	Quantity of Lime to Beadded (gm)
1.	5.00	0.125	4.875	12.50	25.00
2.	10.00	0.250	9.750	25.00	50.00
3.	20.00	0.500	19.500	50.00	100.00
4.	30.00	0.750	29.250	75.00	150.00
5.	40.00	1.000	39.000	100.00	200.00
6.	50.00	1.250	48.750	125.00	250.00
7.	60.00	1.500	58.500	150.00	300.00
8.	80.00	2.000	78.000	200.00	400.00
9.	100.00	2.500	97.500	250.00	500.00

Disinfection of Rearing Houses, Appliances etc.

Drench all parts of rearing building inside and outside and appliances uniformly using gutter or jet sprayer with required quantity of disinfectant (@ 2.0 liter/m^2 floor area of rearing house + 25 per cent of disinfectant solution for appliances + 10 per cent for outside of the building). After disinfection, rearing houses must be closed for a minimum period of 24 hrs. Rearing trays, leaf basket and cocoon storage trays should not be smeared with cow dung. Disinfected rearing houses must be opened at least 24 hrs before arrival of silkworm eggs from grainages.

Dipping the Appliances in Disinfectant

Disinfect the rearing appliances in 2 per cent bleaching powder in 0.3 per cent slaked lime solution by dipping for at least 10 minutes in disinfection tank. The disinfection tank of 2 feet depth and 4 feet diameter is considered suitable for disinfection purpose. Prepare the disinfectant solution of required quantity and concentration and fill half of the tank. To determine the volume of the tank and the disinfectant solution to be prepared the formula Πr^2h is used. Example –

- The volume of tank of 4 feet diameter and 2 feet height.
- Diameter = 4 feet and therefore radius (r) = 4 ÷ 2 = 2; as only half of the tank is to be filled, the height of solution in the tank will be 2 ÷ 2 = 1'.
- Therefore, $\Pi r^2h = 3.14 \times 2 \times 2 \times 1 = 12.56$ cubic feet.
- One cubic feet holds 28 liters of solution, therefore 12.56 cubic feet will hold 12.56 × 28 = 352 liters of solution.

To prepare 352 liters of 2 per cent bleaching powder in 0.3 per cent slaked lime solution, the requirement will be as follows:

- Requirement of water = 352 liters
- Requirement of bleaching powder = 352 × 20 gm = 7.040 kg.
- Requirement of 0.3 per cent slaked lime = 352 × 3 gm = 1.056 kg.

Prepare 352 liters of solution and fill in the disinfection tank. Dip the appliances as many as possible to submerge in the solution. After 10 minutes the appliances are removed from the disinfection tank and carried directly to the disinfected rearing houses. Afterwards, another set of appliances is dipped in the solution. This system will continue for 8-10 times. The solution is discarded after using 10 times and fresh solution is prepared for the purpose.

Maintenance of hygienic conditions is ensured by rigorous practice of disinfection on the vulnerable foci of infection. Disinfection of rearing room and appliances to prevent vertical transmission of pathogens is very much essential which is to be carried out before rearing operation with available disinfectants to destroy pathogens. Disinfection of other sources of contamination/infection to prevent horizontal transmission of pathogens is –

- Surface sterilization of silkworm eggs after received at rearing establishments.
- Disinfection of rearing rooms/building.
- Disinfection of surrounding areas of rearing building.
- Disinfection of rearing appliances.
- Personal hygiene.

Before to use the disinfectants, it is of utmost importance to think about the residual effect of the disinfectants towards environmental pollution and positive side effects on the persons who are handling the disinfectants as also their pets. As no disinfectant is absolutely free from the above, only those disinfectants are to be selected where the side effects are minimal. At present Chlorine dioxide ranks first being the most eco-friendly and users friendly disinfectant available to the sericulture industry. Regular practice of disinfection in all possible ways has proved to be very much effective to maintain hygiene and its successful implementation will minimize crop loss due to diseases.

- *Effectiveness of Disinfectants:* The effectiveness of disinfectant chemical depends mainly on three factors *i.e.,* concentration, duration of treatment and ambient temperature at the time of disinfection.

Schedule of Disinfection

The disinfection of rearing establishments and appliances with disinfectants are to be carried out systematically as per recommendation to prevent the contamination and diseases during silkworm rearing for healthy growth of larvae and to harvest stable cocoon crop. The recommendation is presented in Table 3.7.

Table 3.7: Schedule of Disinfectants (Rajan and Himantharaj, 2005)

Day	Activity	Details of Activity
After the completion of previous rearing	1	Collection and burning of diseased larvae, melted and flimsy cocoons.
	2	Disinfection of mountages.
	3	1st disinfection of rearing house and appliances with 2 per cent bleaching powder in 0.3 per cent slaked lime solution or Sanitech/Serichlor 2.5 per cent in slaked lime 0.5 per cent.
5 days before brushing	4	Cleaning and washing of rearing house and appliances.
	5	Sun drying of appliances.
4 days before brushing	6	Optional disinfection of rearing establishment with 0.3 per cent slaked lime.
3 days before brushing	7	2nd disinfection of rearing house and appliances with 2 per cent bleaching powder in 0.3 per cent slaked lime solution or Sanitech/Serichlor 2.5 per cent in slaked lime 0.5 per cent.
2 days before brushing	8	Dusting disinfectant (5% bleaching powder in slaked lime) @ 200 gm per square meter at the entrance of rearing house, surroundings and to the passage.
	9	Open the window of rearing house for ventilation to drive off the odour of disinfectant. Prevent the entry of unauthorized person into the rearing room.
1 day before brushing	10	Preparation of brushing and maintain hygiene

Maintenance of Hygiene

- Do not borrow rearing appliances.
- Do not use rearing appliances without disinfection.
- Avoid overlapping rearing operations.
- Dead eggs should be separated from the batch received for rearing and subjected for microscopical examination.
- Disinfect the silkworm eggs with 2 per cent formalin for 5-10 minutes and wash with clean water, dry them in shade as soon as received from grainages to the rearing sites. Disinfect also before initiation of incubation.
- Hand gloves, aprons and foot wears should be used while handling silkworm larvae.
- Maintain personnel and rearing hygiene throughout rearing operation.
- Restrict the entry of persons in the rearing house.
- Silkworm testing area (disease examination place) should be properly disinfected every day before and after carrying out the microscopical examination of larvae.
- At the passage of entrance to rearing building, sprinkle 5 per cent bleaching powder in slaked lime @ 18 gm/sq. ft.
- Rearers or any other person involved in rearing operation entering to the rearing rooms must disinfect foot and hand before entry. Hand should be thoroughly washed with alkaline germicidal soap.
- The foot mat place at the entrance of rearing building is to be soaked in 2 per cent bleaching powder in 0.3 per cent slaked lime solution. The foot mat must be soaked in disinfectant solution daily.
- Separate footwear and clean apron should be used.
- Wipe the floor daily after bed cleaning with 2 per cent bleaching powder in 0.3 per cent slaked lime solution. If the floor is of mud, dust 5 per cent bleaching powder in slaked lime at an interval of 3-4 days without fail.
- Silkworm testing equipments such as crushing sets, mixie cups, glass rods, beakers, funnels etc., should be cleaned and disinfected after every sample examination.

Table 3.8: Disinfectants and their Requirement for 200 sq. ft., floor area of Rearing Building

Item to Disinfectant	Mode of Disinfection	Quantity Required	Quantity of Disinfectants Required		
			Bleaching Powder (kg)	Slaked Lime (kg)	Detergent (kg)
Rearing house (200 sq. ft. or 18.58 sq. mtr) and appliances (8 rearing stands and 160 trays).	Spray disinfection, cleaning and washing with 2 per cent bleaching powder in 0.3 per cent slaked lime + 50 per cent for appliances.	Floor area of rearing house × 2 liters/sq. mtr + 50 per cent for appliances *i.e.* 18.58 × 2 = 37.00 + 18.50 liters = 55.5 liters.	1.11	0.166	—
Disinfection of rearing appliances by soaking the trays, plastic sheets etc.	2 per cent bleaching powder in 0.3 per cent slaked lime solution.	500 liters.	10.00	1.500	—
Spray disinfection of rearing house and surroundings.	0.3 per cent slaked lime solution + 25 per cent for surroundings.	37 liters + 9.25 liters = 46.25 liters.	—	0.138	—
Spray disinfection of rearing house and appliances.	2 per cent formalin + 0.5 per cent detergent + 50 per cent for appliances + 25 per cent for rearing house and surroundings.	37 liters + 18.5 liters + 9.25 liters = 64.75 liters or 65.00 liters.	—	—	0.325

- The rearing staff should properly be trained in different procedures of disinfections and maintenance of hygiene.
- Rear silkworm always on rearing sheet papers/news paper and change it as and when soiled.
- Compost pit should always be away from the rearing house.
- Diseased larvae from the rearing bed and non-spinning larvae from the mountages should be picked and disposed off in 2 per cent bleaching powder in 0.3 per cent slaked lime solution.
- Feed sufficient quantity of good quality mulberry leaves for robust larval growth. Provide recommended spacing and sufficient ventilation for healthy growth of later instar larvae.
- Mulberry leaves should not be stored on the rearing room. Instead stored it in separate disinfected room.
- Dust the bed disinfectant as recommended.
- Cocoons should not be stored nearby the rearing houses and separate stored room should be provided for them.

CHAPTER 4

Incubations

Quality silkworm seed is the basic requirement of the sericulture industry. The crop performance and silk productivity are directly related to the quality of seed. It is very difficult to define the term 'Quality of silkworm seed' but for all practical purposes, the quality silkworm seed can be considered as eggs produced from good cocoons under optimal environmental conditions. Quality can deteriorate due to improper handling during its processing, preservation, hibernation, acid treatment, chilling, incubation, transportation etc. Incubation is one of the most important techniques in egg handling. Incubation is an acclaimed important step to obtain uniform hatching, normal growth of larvae and good quality of stable cocoon crop (Das and Sengupta, 1991). Therefore, the term incubation can be defined as preservation of silkworm eggs under optimum environmental conditions of temperature (25 ± 2^{0}C), RH (75 ± 5%) and photoperiod (16 L: 8 D) during embryonic development, so as to suit the silkworm eggs to develop normally to provide uniform and maximum hatchability on the expected day. The term incubation is used especially to those eggs, which are naturally active or artificially activated and not to those eggs, which are kept under aestivation. Thus, incubation of silkworm eggs is conducted under manipulated micro-environmental conditions, which enables them to develop normally.

Objectives of Incubation

Incubation aims at –

1. To promote proper development ensuring that eggs of different breeds/hybrids should hatch on the desired date and time and it should be more than 90 per cent on a single day.
2. To enforce uniform hatching at a specific time to produce healthy silkworm larvae and ultimately stable cocoon crop.
3. To maintain the voltinism of the breed.
4. To stabilize the hibernating characters and hibernating potency value of the bivoltine eggs.
5 To maintain uniform larval growth for harvestation of successful cocoon crop.

Types of Incubation

Incubation is of three types –

(i) *Interruption Incubation:* In the interruption method, the temperature at the beginning of incubation is kept at 15-18^{0}C and after one or two days the incubation is allowed for four days at 22-23^{0}C up to blastokinesis stage. At the final stage of incubation, the temperature is maintained at 25^{0}C until hatching.

(ii) *Progressive Incubation:* In the progressive incubation method, the temperature in the beginning is maintained at lower level and thereafter it is kept constant around 25^{0}C until hatching.

(iii) *Kyuri Incubation:* This method is not in practice now-a-days as the technique of artificial hatching method is well adopted. However, in this method the temperature in the beginning is maintained at 20-23^{0}C and during the development of embryo when thoracic appendages

appear or just before the blastokinesis, the temperature is brought down to 15⁰C. This condition is continued until just before hatching. At the time of hatching once again, the temperature is increased to 24-25⁰C. This incubation method is adopted when it is necessary to obtain non-diapause eggs.

Methods of Incubation

Incubation is carried out generally by two methods –

(i) Constant temperature incubation.

(ii) Raised temperature incubation.

In constant temperature incubation method, incubation is carried out at a constant temperature of 25-26⁰C from beginning to till hatching. This method is practiced for acid treated and non-hibernated eggs. Raised temperature incubation method is used for incubation of hibernating eggs. The hibernating eggs soon after release from cold storages are preserved at 10-15⁰C for 3 days, 18-20⁰C for 2 days; 23-24⁰C for 4 days and 25-26⁰C till hatching. This avoids sudden shock of temperature to delicate silkworm eggs and helps in uniform development of embryos and hatching. However, generally, constant temperature incubation is in practice.

Devices for Silkworm Egg Incubation

Incubation can be practiced by adopting one of the following techniques –

- *Room Incubation:* In places where cold storages are available, exclusive incubation rooms are constructed for incubation of silkworm eggs in large quantities. These rooms have provision of maintaining optimum uniform temperature and humidity conditions, provision of regulating the photoperiod besides good ventilation. Incubation rooms should not be overcrowded with silkworm eggs as it increases the carbon-dioxide content during embryo development.
- *Mud Pot Incubation:* Mud pot incubation is ideal for individual farmers for incubation of 250-300 Dfls. The

well baked earthen pot with a wide mouth of 15" diameter is chosen. The mud pot is filled with a clean sand layer of 2-3" thick and made wet depending on the need and requirement. It is provided with a row of holes of about half an inch diameter situated 2-3" above the sand level. The pot is covered with wet muslin cloth. The laying is hanged inside the pot with the help of a rod and the pot is placed over an ant well. Monitor the cloth/sand regularly for wetness. As a result the temperature is generally reduced by 5-10^{0}C. Mud pot incubation can be utilised whenever temperature prevails higher than optimum. It is more suitable method of incubation in hot and arid (dry) areas.

- *Double Brick Walled Incubation Chamber*: This method of incubation is suitable for individual grainages, CRCs and big sericulture farmers. The chamber is constructed using brunt bricks, sand and cement. Gap of 3" is maintained between outer and inner walls. The gap is filled with loose clean sand. The standard size of outer wall is 6′ × 4′ × 3′ and inner wall 4′ × 2′ × 3′ with a gap of 3" between them. This incubation device can accommodate 5000-6000 Dfls. The egg sheets are hanged in the chamber with sufficient gap between them. The sand layer is soaked periodically with water depending upon the prevailing environmental conditions during incubation. The temperature and humidity can be maintained to near optimum conditions by this method. This method of incubation is suitable during summer months.
- *Tray Incubation:* The eggs can be incubated in clean rearing tray in which wet foam pads are placed at the periphery and covered with paraffin paper. During favourable seasons, the silkworm egg sheets are spread in the rearing trays for incubation. The rooms should be heated with the help of electric heater up to the required optimum temperature. Boiling water in wide mouthed vessel on charcoal stove can increase humidity. This helps in increasing temperature and humidity both.

- *Incubation in Incubator*: In India, to maintain the required temperature and humidity for incubation, the silkworm eggs are incubated in BOD incubator. Incubators with light facility can also be used for incubation of silkworm eggs. The temperature in incubator is set to the required level and humidity is maintained by keeping a tray of water inside the incubator preferably at the bottom.

Factors Associated with Incubation

The main factors related to incubation of silkworm eggs are disinfections, transportation, temperature, relative humidity, photoperiod, aeration and black boxing, which determine the various activities of life and success of silkworm crop (Rao *et al.* 1998).

Disinfection

Rooms and equipments where incubation has to be carried out should be thoroughly disinfected prior to commencement of incubation. Silkworm eggs should be surface sterilized with 2 per cent formalin for 10-15 minutes before and after cold storage of eggs.

Transportation

Various commodities are transported daily by various means, but egg transportation has to be carried out with all care and diligence in all conditions, which foster continued healthy growth of silkworm. It is emphasised that maintenance of recommended temperature and humidity is very crucial during transportation of eggs from cold storages/grainages to incubation centres. The transportation of silkworm eggs has to be carried out by providing optimum environmental conditions of temperature (25 ± 1^0C) and humidity ($75 \pm 5\%$) to exploit the full potential of the breed/hybrid. If eggs are exposed to unfavourable conditions for longer duration, it would have a tremendous impact on the developing embryos which may cause irreparable damage. Once, the damage is inflicted, the silkworm eggs being a closed system can not circumvent the imposition of nature and the penalty is imminent. The implications would be mortality of the developing embryos, poor and irregular hatching, weaker hatched larvae and loss of weight in the newly hatched larvae and consequent death in 2-3 days after brushing, susceptibility to diseases and increased early stage loss. Temperature of 25 + 1^{0}C even though ideal during transportation of eggs but it becomes dangerous when RH is 35 per cent or less. It not only affects hatching but also retards growth and extend incubation period. Under acute hostile conditions, the embryo could collapse in the mid-course of development or may extend its lease of life up to pin-head/blue egg stage and die. On the other hand, if RH is too high *i.e.* 90 per cent and above, it leads to retention of water, a product of oxidation of nutrients and poisons the embryos. Such embryos develop into weaker larvae and become easily susceptible to diseases. Therefore, silkworm eggs has to be transported by providing the nearest optimum temperature and RH. It is recommended to transport eggs during cooler hours of the day using egg carrying bag or box in order to provide required temperature and RH equilibrium. Efforts (Rajan and Himanthraj, 2005) should be made to avoid –

- Exposure of eggs to direct sun light and high temperature.
- Transportation of eggs in sealed boxes without perforations.
- Storing of eggs in enclosed places with poor ventilation.
- Direct or indirect contact of eggs with tobacco or poisonous chemicals.
- Contamination of eggs with pathogens.
- Exposure of eggs to fumes, fertilizers, petroleum and insecticides.
- Physical shocks to eggs.

It is advisable to transport silkworm eggs during early developmental stages and at the time when temperature fluctuation is less *i.e.*, during morning or evening time specially by keeping them in transportation boxes designed and fabricated for the purpose.

Temperature

Temperature during incubation is one of the most important factors that play a vital role and decides the growth and development of embryos, uniformity of hatching, hatching per cent, vigour of larvae and quality of cocoons besides voltinism. Although the embryonic development takes place between 10-30^{0}C but their development is not uniform leading to irregular hatching over a period of time. The optimum temperature of 25 ± 1^{0}C is ideal for incubation at which the embryonic growth is normal. Any fluctuation from the optimum during incubation affects the development of embryos. The relation between incubation temperature and time required for hatching is presented in Table 4.1.

Table 4.1: Incubation Temperature and Time Required for Hatching

S. No.	Incubation Temperature (^{0}C)	Incubation Duration (days)
1.	10	70-80
2.	15	30-33
3.	2.0	15-16
4.	25	9-10
5.	30	8-9

Temperature above 30^{0}C is highly deleterious as hatching is significantly affected, and at 33^{0}C hatching is almost negligible. Among the developmental stages, the silkworm egg stage has the lowest tolerance to high temperature. Temperature during incubation also affects voltinism character as the embryonic stages are most sensitive to it. Bivoltine eggs incubated at 25^{0}C and above produce moths that lay hibernated eggs, while those incubated at temperature below 25^{0}C produce moths that lay mixed and fully non-hibernated eggs (20^{0}C mixed and 15^{0}C non-hibernated eggs). Developmental rate is directly influenced by temperature and modified by humidity. At high temperature embryos grow faster up to the setae formation stage and succumbs to death as yolk can not be utilised in pace with the high rate of development which comes in the way of normal development (Yamashita and Hasegawa, 1985). Silkworm eggs during course of its development under optimal conditions show approximately 12 per cent weight loss. This loss is due to the oxidation of nutrients required for the growth of the embryo during which metabolic water, CO_2 and energy are released (Reddy *et al.* 2005). Temperature above 30°C results in abnormal weight loss which leads to desiccation of eggs affecting hatching per cent. Influence of order of egg maturation on weight of eggs, glycogen and water contents (moisture) in newly laid eggs of silkworm is presented by Reddy *et al.* 2005 (Table 4.2). It is established that embryos can tolerate high temperature during the first two days of incubation, but higher temperature for more than two days killed embryos.

Table 4.2: Influence of Order of Egg Maturation in Bivoltine Silkworm Breeds of NB_4D_2

S. No.	Time of Oviposition	No. of Eggs/gm	Weight of Eggs (mg)	Moisture %	Glycogen (mg/ gm wet weight)
1.	4 pm-5 pm	1670	0.59	63.40	20.93
2.	5 pm-6 pm	1750	0.57	62.86	23.18
3.	6 pm-10 pm	1750	0.57	62.79	33.15
4.	10 pm-10 am	1820	0.55	61.52	31.91
5.	10 am-10 pm (2nd day)	1820	0.55	61.21	32.68
	Average	1762	0.57	62.36	23.37

Humidity

Humidity is an important factor, which directly affects the physiology of silkworm eggs. Too dry or too wet air is harmful to the physiology of developing embryos. The humidity range of 70-80 per cent is ideal for maintaining the normal development of silkworm eggs. Humidity less than 60 per cent results in loss of water from silkworm eggs and humidity of 90 per cent and above leads to retention of physiological waste water resulting in poisoning of embryos.

Humidity in combination with temperature has very strong effect on the developmental physiology of eggs. Though a temperature of 25 ± 1^{0}C is ideal for incubation but if humidity is as low as 30 ± 5 per cent, the ideal temperature itself becomes dangerous for the development of eggs. It not only affects hatching but also retards growth and prolongs the incubation period. Low humidity during pinhead and blue egg stage makes the gluey substance that covers the eggs rather hard as cement and the larvae find it difficult to bite the eggshell and eventually fail to hatch. A combination of high temperature and low humidity, results in desiccation and majority of eggs fail to hatch. The weight of newly hatched larvae decreases significantly when incubated at low humidity and high temperature due to desiccation and improper utilisation of yolk. If humidity increases to 90-100 per cent during incubation, weak trimoulter larvae silkworm appears during rearing. Recommended temperature and humidity during incubation of silkworm eggs is presented in Table 4.3.

Table 4.3: Recommended Temperature and Humidity during Incubation of Eggs

Type of Eggs	Temperature	Duration	Humidity
Acid treated eggs	24-26^0 C	Up to hatching	75 ± 5%
Hibernated eggs	15^0 C	3 Days	
	24-26^0 C	Up to hatching	

Photoperiod

Photoperiod has a direct effect on hatching and voltinism during incubation period in the Bivoltine silkworms. From the very beginning of incubation up to the eye spot stage, light hastens the embryonic development. However, during final hatching stage, darkness inhibits development. In darkness, the eggs can be inhibited from hatching upto 9 hours only and there after they start to hatch regardless of darkness. These eggs waiting to hatch in the darkness are very sensitive to light and even dim light when provided for short duration results in good hatching per cent. Bivoltine silkworm eggs should be incubated at 16 hrs lights and 8 hrs dark to maintain the diapausing nature in the ensuing generation. The intensity of light on egg surface should be above 10 lux. In case of low temperature incubation, the eggs are kept in darkness throughout the day or the light conditions per day should not exceed 12 hrs. If eggs are allowed to remain under light conditions throughout the day, the hatching will not be uniform. The most critical stage of the embryo, which is sensitive to photoperiod, is from the stage of appearance of thoracic appendages. In order to obtain maximum hatching within a short period, the eggs in eye spot stage are kept in darkness and on the day of hatching, they are suddenly brought out to bright light conditions.

Aeration

Since the eggs undergoing incubation respire vigorously, the room should be airy, so that there is no hindrance to free respiration. Aeration from the middle of the incubation plays very important role. Good ventilation provides good circulation of air, which helps in driving out poisonous gases produced due to metabolic activity of silkworm eggs. If carbon dioxide content is less than 0.5 per cent, it does no harm to the developing embryos but when it exceeds this level becomes deleterious and kills the developing eggs. Therefore, incubation room should be properly ventilated or aerated particularly during later stage of incubation.

Black Boxing of Silkworm Eggs

Black boxing technique provides synchronized hatching on a single day and within in a short period. The eggs, which are not black boxed, hatches irregularly over a period of time. In order to obtain synchronized hatching in a short period, photoperiod is manipulated during the later stage of egg development especially at the time when egg development reaches to pinhead stage (head pigmentation stage), the eggs are subjected for complete darkness known as 'scotophase' and exposed to light after 48 hrs. This procedure is based on the fact that faster egg development takes place in the light up to head pigmentation stage and darkness enhances uniform development from pinhead stage up to onset of hatching. This technique of providing complete darkness to developing embryos from pinhead stage to the onset of hatching is known as 'black boxing technique'. It has twin advantages –

- To force late maturing or lagging embryos to accelerate their development and join there developed counterparts.
- The insects being photosensitive in nature, darkness inhibits hatching process largely. This inhibition is intricately related to the 'biological clock' operating in the nervous system.

Methods of Black Boxing

The methods of black boxing are –

- *Dark Room Method*: The entire room where silkworm eggs are incubated can be made dark by switching off the lights when eggs reached to head pigmentation stage and exposed to light only after 48 hrs.
- *Incubator Method*: The silkworm eggs are incubated in total darkness in incubators till they reach head pigmentation stage and exposed to light only after 48 hrs.
- *Black Cloth Method*: The silkworm eggs kept in trays for incubation are covered with double-layered black cloth when developing embryos reaches head pigmentation stage and exposed to light after 48 hrs.
- *Wooden Box Method*: A wooden box painted on inner side with black paint can be effectively used for incubation. Foam pads or wet cloths or wet paper can be kept on the floor of the box to increase the humidity if required. Eggs after reaching to head pigmentation stage are kept in these boxes and exposed to light after 48 hrs.
- *Black Paper Method:* The silkworm eggs are kept in black paper cover, which are sealed by using clips to avoid entry of light. The clips are opened and eggs are exposed to light after 48 hrs on the expected day of hatching.

Effect of Incubation Environment on Voltinism

The major environmental factors affecting voltinism are –

Temperature

Temperature during incubation has greatest influence on voltinism. In other words, temperature during incubation plays an important role in determining that whether Bivoltine silkworms will lay hibernating or non-hibernating eggs. When Bivoltine eggs are incubated at a temperature of 25⁰C or above, the resulting moths will lay hibernating eggs, and when incubated at a low temperature of 15⁰C, they will lay non-hibernating eggs regardless of environmental conditions during larval and pupal stages. An intermediate temperature of 20⁰C during incubation will result in production of mixture of hibernating and non-hibernating eggs (Table 4.4).

Table 4.4: Influence of Temperature during Incubation on Various Stages of Development of Bivoltine Silkworm

Incubation Stage	Grown Larval Stage	Mounting/ Pupal Stage	Voltinism of Eggs Laid
High temperature (Above 25⁰C)	High temperature (Above 25⁰C)	High temperature (Above 25⁰C)	Hibernating
	Low temperature (18⁰C)	Low temperature (20⁰C)	Non-hibernating
Low temperature (15⁰C)	High temperature (Above 25⁰C)	High temperature (Above 28⁰C)	Non-hibernating
	Low temperature (18⁰C)	Low temperature (20⁰C)	Non-hibernating
Intermediate temperature (Above 20⁰C)	High temperature (Above 25⁰C)	High temperature (Above 28⁰C)	Mostly Non-hibernating
	Low temperature (18⁰C)	Low temperature (20⁰C)	Mostly Non-hibernating

Photoperiod

Light during incubation also influences voltinism but the effect is not evident if temperature is above 25⁰C or below 15⁰C. At the intermediate temperature, if long photoperiod is provided to the developing embryos, the resulting moths will lay higher rate of hibernating eggs. On the contrast, the short photoperiod induces more non-hibernating eggs. It is established that the influence of light is next to temperature.

Humidity

The influence of humidity on voltinism is next to light. Humidity does not affect voltinism if incubation temperature is above 25^{0}C or below 15^{0}C. At intermediate incubation temperature, high humidity is favourable for inducing more hibernating eggs, while low humidity favors non-hibernating eggs. Temperature, light and humidity affect the voltinism of silkworms at the stage between when embryo begins to form the thoracic legs and when the head begins to be pigmented. The basic requirement for the Bivoltine to lay hibernating eggs is a temperature above 25^{0}C. If eggs are incubated at a temperature below 15^{0}C and kept in dark and dry condition, most of the Bivoltine races may produce non-hibernating eggs in the resulting moths.

Cold Storage of Blue Eggs and New Born Larvae

Hatching of eggs during incubation can be delayed by cold storing the eggs at blue egg stage at 5^{0}C for 3-5 days. Newly hatched larvae if necessary can be cold stored for 3 days at 7-10^{0}C. The humidity in the cold storage room should be maintained at 75-80 per cent.

Rotten Eggs before Head Pigmentation

Sometimes rotten eggs such as brown rot, red rot and grey rot eggs are observed during incubation period. Several factors are responsible for such type of damage of eggs –

- Exposure of eggs to high temperature (> 28^{0}C) and high humidity (> 90%) during oviposition and incubation.
- Storage of hibernating eggs for too long period under dry and high temperature conditions.
- Over stimulation of hibernating eggs during acid treatment.
- Contact of eggs by pesticides, nicotine, mosquito repellant, incense, oil or sticky material such as glue or gum.

Dead Eggs after Head Pigmentation

During incubation, two types of embryo death can be observed *i.e.*, one at head pigmentation stage and the other when eggs ready to turn bluish. In these cases, embryo is normally formed but the death occurs before hatching due to –

- Too high temperature during incubation (> 28^0C).
- Too low relative humidity during incubation (< 50%). This condition while causing death of the embryo, also results in stray hatching (un-uniform hatching) and under weight of newly born larvae.
- Contact of eggs with pesticides, nicotine, mosquito repellant, incense or other toxic materials.

Development of Silkworm Eggs During Incubation

When the silkworm eggs are transferred to incubation centres, they are mostly in organogenesis stage of development which is reached at the end of approximately 2 days of oviposition. At this stage, neural groove appears in embryos (Stage 16, non-diapause). Appendages development in gnathal and thoracic regions starts at the very next stage (Stage 17). After three days of oviposition, abdominal limb buds are formed from third to sixth abdominal segments (Stage 18). Paired gonad analages also appears at the same time. Next stage of development indicates beginning of embryo shortening (Stage 19), invagination of spiracles and silk glands besides formation of strand like gonad analages. After four days of oviposition, the head and thorax becomes differentiated (Stage 20), with the grouping of gnathal appendages.

The anterior six segments of embryo fuse together to form the head. During fusion, two segments disappears and thus leaving four in the head region. Thoracic appendages develop into three segmented legs. In the abdominal region, except the five pairs of appendages, which persists later in the larva, remaining disappears during the course of development. Last three segments of the abdomen fuse together to form single segment and thus leaving abdomen with only nine segments. Blastokinesis begins at this stage.

Actually, blastokinesis is the characteristic of all those insects whose eggs are rich in yolk and the germ band is invaginated therein. Blastokinesis occurs 4-5 days after oviposition. The embryo starts to move around as it seeks its correct position in the egg (Stage 21A, B & C). For instance the embryo, which was in the supine position with its abdomen facing outer of the egg turns round, so that its abdomen faces the inner side. This whole process is called blastokinesis. The anterior and posterior ectodermal invaginations (stomodaeum and proctodaeum) forms the fore intestine and hind intestine respectively. During this stage, the embryo, located on the ventral side of the egg, moves towards the dorsal side.

After blastokinesis, histogenesis proceeds actively and continues till the larva hatches. The first embryonic molt takes place just after blastokinesis followed by second molt immediately, after which the larval cuticle is secreted (Stage 24). After revolution, various organs are gradually formed and eggs hatch in about 5 days later. The number of embryonic segment in *B. mori* is reported to be 18. Of these, four anterior segments form the head, three segments form the thorax and the other eleven segments form the abdomen.

Mesoderm cells, forms four pairs of appendages on the head region and three pairs on the thoracic region. Besides these seven pairs of appendages, the mesodermic cells also form one pair of appendage on each of the eleven abdominal segments. Of these eleven pairs of appendages on the abdominal region, only 3rd, 4th, 5th, 6th and 11th abdominal segments appendages develop further and remaining six pairs disappear during the course of development (Stage 18).

While antenna, skin, mouth parts, thoracic leg, abdominal leg, caudal leg, silk gland and other dermo-glands besides fore and hind intestine, nervous system, trachea, sense organs, malphigian tube and external genetalia are formed from ectodermal cells, internal genetalia, muscles, dorsal vessels, sub-esophageal gland, corpuscles, pericardial cells, fat tissues originate from mesoderm. In diapausing embryos, cell division is arrested and embryogenesis ceases immediately after formation of the cephalic lobe and segmentation of mesoderm. Yolk cells and yolk granules change their shape and properties as a part of diapause process. The most striking feature of the diapausing eggs is the dark colouration of serosal cells due to the formation of ommochrome pigment. When diapause is terminated (Stage 15), embryogenesis resumes and follows the pattern as in non-diapause eggs. Further, in diapausing eggs, stage of development from 16 onwards is delayed approximately one day in comparison to non-diapausing eggs. Developmental events occurring during incubation of silkworm eggs are presented in Table 4.5 (Tazima, 1978; Singh *et al.* 2002; Singh and Saratchandra, 2004; Singh *et al.* 2010).

Stage of Black Boxing

Silkworm eggs should be black boxed when majority of eggs (80%) has reached to head pigmentation stage. Black boxing of eggs at body pigmentation stage (blue egg stage) is not ideal, as light stimulus would have already been perceived by the brain cells of embryos, as a result hatching will be initiated inside the black box itself (Rao *et al.* 1998). The head pigmentation stage is identified by a small black dot in the eggs near the micropylar end. The black spot appears mostly on the 7th day in multivoltine breeds and on the 8th day in Bivoltine breeds under optimum incubation conditions.

Duration of Black Boxing

The period of black boxing depends on the stage of embryo prior to black boxing. In multivoltines, the pigmented stage can easily be identified; as such 48 hrs black boxing is sufficient for synchronized developments and hatching. However, in Bivoltine, the change of color of egg to pin-head stage is not clearly visible due to the pigmented serosa and requires expertise in identifying the stage. The appearance of head pigmentation and consumption of serosa are simultaneous process. After complete consumption of serosa, the pin head becomes clearly visible. Thus eggs can be black boxed for 72 hrs after the appearance of head pigmentation

Table 4.5: Developmental Events during Incubation of Silkworm Eggs

S. No.	Tempt. (^{0}C)	Stage of Embryo	Physio-Morphological Status of Silkworm Eggs
1	2	3	4
1.	25	Incubation Stage (Organogenesis) (Stage 16)	16 hrs light and 8 hrs dark/day to maintain bivoltine characters; starts losing 1-2 per cent of water per day. Hence maintain 75 ± 5 per cent RH to avoid desiccation; within 0.5 hr after shifting from 15^{0}C to 25^{0}C the neural groove appears; starts gradual increase in oxygen consumption. This stage is commonly called incubation stage.
2.	25	Stage 17 (1.5-2 days)	Appendages appear in the form of buds in the protocephalon, gnathal and thoracic region. Segmentation of the body region is clearly visible. From this stage onwards 400-500 lux light with 100 cm distance is to be provided.
3.	25	Stage 18 (2.5-3rd day)	Mandible, maxillary, labial and three thoracic segments become clear. Stomodaeam is clearly visible. 4 pairs of abdominal buds are seen from 3-6 abdominal segments.
4.	25	Stage 19 (3rd day)	The labial and antennal rudiments appear as paired hemispherical lobes. Thoracic legs show segmentation. Shortening of embryo.
5.	25	Stage 20 (3rd-4th day)	Further development of appendages, head and thorax distinguishable, embryo is further shortened, better to transport the eggs before attaining the blastokinesis stage.
6.	25	Stage 21 (A, B and C) (4.5-5th day)	Morphogenetic movement of embryo, early, middle and late blastokinesis, completion of dorsal closure.

Contd...

1	2	3	4
7.	25	Stage 22 (5th day)	Complete embryonic reversal (blastokinesis completed). Morphogenetic movement of the cephalognathal region begins to form head.
8.	25	Stage 23 (6th day)	Thoracic and abdominal appendages clearly visible. Steep rise in oxygen consumption and CO_2 release.
9.	25	Stage 24 (7th day)	Tubercles appear on the body of the embryo. Setae formation. Abdominal legs clawed, caudal horns also develop.
10.	25	Stage 25 (7th day)	Formation of taenidia inside the tracheae and tracheal, initiation of sperm tube formation.
11.	25	Stage 26 (8th day) (head pigmentation-I)	Up to 0.5 per cent CO_2 in air tolerable, beyond this causes uneven development, irregular and delayed hatching, head capsule darkening.
12.	25	Stage 28 (9th day) (early body pigmentation)	Darkening of thorax and abdomen, dark coloration helps in obtaining the synchronized hatching stage.
13.	25	Stage 29 (10th day) (late body pigmentation)	More darkened body, young larva completed, Sensitive to low RH and high CO_2 level, hence eggs may die in this stage.
14.	25	Stage 30 (10th-11th day)	Hatching of young larvae within 2-3 hrs after light exposure.

stage. However, if uniform head pigmentation in majority of eggs are observed, they can be black boxed for 48 hrs and then exposed to light.

Light Exposure to Stimulate Hatching

A photoperiod of 16 hrs light and 8 hrs darkness during incubation up to pin-head stage and then shifting to darkness and later sudden exposure to bright illumination enable uniform hatching. The hatching date can be determined by the embryonic development with reference to the color of the egg and distinctness of the egg dimple. Hatching occurs within 2-3 hrs after exposure to light. The laying from the dark phase is exposed to bright light at about 6 A. M. In the absence of electricity, the eggs can be brought under natural light. A relative humidity of 70 per cent is ideal at the time of hatching.

If or any reason, the hatching is to be delayed after incubation has started, it can be done to a limited period by cold storing the eggs at 5^0C on the second or third day of incubation for about one week. Hatching can also be delayed at blue egg stage by cold storing for about a week at 5^0C.

- *Respiration through Eggshell:* Respiration is a fundamental biological phenomenon necessary for the maintenance of biochemical reactions, which are the characteristic of the living systems. The gas exchange process is passive and is based upon diffusion governed by co-efficient and relative partial pressure of oxygen on either side of the eggshell. Respiratory canals are funnel shaped tubes, which becomes narrower as it enters inward. These respiratory canals are aeropyles and are responsible for gas exchange process during embryogenesis. These aeropyles are tiny holes transversing relatively thick chorion and conducting the ambient air directly to the trabecular layer and from there to the oocyte. These aeropyles functions during embryogenesis in gas exchange as per 'Bernoulli Velocity Gradients Theory'. The aeropyles are distributed in large numbers over the entire surface of the egg except around the micropyle.

Structurally, aeropyle openings are somehow elevated or surrounded by crowns. These respiratory devices carry the ambient air to the internal trabecular layer for both storage and immediate consumption. Oxygen moves within the trabecular layer and cross the inner layers (endochorion and vitelline membrane) and reaches to the developing oocyte. The inner membranes are structurally porous, so that the oxygen can pass through, where the metabolic processes are taking place. Moreover, if the ambient environment is poor in oxygen, having a partial pressure lower than that within the embryo; it may prove fatal for the development. Carbon dioxide is driven easily from inside, since its partial pressure in the environment is virtually zero.

Since, the oxygen and carbon dioxide molecules are bigger than the water molecules; it was not possible for biological systems to evolve a kind of membrane, which would be permeable only to oxygen and carbon dioxide, but not to water. Hence, the loss in water content during embryogenesis cannot be ruled out. Number of workers has described the phenomenon of gradual loss in weight of fertilized eggs during the course of their embryonic development. Therefore, the weight of silkworm eggs is not a constant factor during the course of development. The maximum loss in weight of eggs has been reported on the day of hatching. The loss in weight of eggs in the course of embryogenesis is partly due to the exhalation of carbon dioxide and partly due to the loss in moisture content (Mathur and Singh, 1990). The difference in egg weight is also due to energy loss during embryogenesis.

Embryo Isolation

Embryological studies in sericulturally advanced countries are well practiced. It is a technology aimed in solving practical problems related to identification of suitable embryonic stages in order to develop an effective and efficient model for long-term preservation of silkworm eggs. The eggs are to be handled in accordance to their embryonic stages to maintain or retain the potency or viability, as each stage has its own tolerance limits for temperature and humidity conditions.

Embryo isolation technique is very crucial in monitoring and identifying the different stages of development of eggs during aestivation, hibernation, preservation and release from cold storages or re-refrigeration during long-term preservation and incubation.

Advantages of Embryo Isolation

- Helps in long-term preservation of bivoltine as well as multivoltine eggs.
- Helps as an appropriate indicator of time for release of hibernated eggs.
- Helps in handling of eggs in accordance with the need of environmental conditions.
- Helps to forecast the exact date and hatching percentage well in advance.
- Helps in identifying the specific stages which are sensitive or resistant to various egg handling techniques.
- Helps to judge whether eggs are properly handled or not.

Techniques of Embryo Isolation

Different techniques are followed in isolation of embryos for identification of various developmental stages. They are –

(a) *Hot Water Fixation Technique*

- Treat the silkworm eggs in hot water.
- Dry the silkworm eggs under fan.
- Cut the egg shell from the micropyler region laterally using a sharp blade under a dissection stereomicroscope.
- Squirt water with force using Pasteur pipette on cut eggs placed in Petri dish with water to release the embryos.
- Transfer the released embryos carefully onto a microslide.
- Remove the yolk particles if any sticking to the embryos using the soft brush.

- Observe under microscope to identify the stages of embryonic development.
- Permanent slides can be prepared using Borax carmine or Haematoxylin stain.
- In case of loose eggs, the eggs are to be fixed in paraffin wax in Petri dish and cut.

Table 4.6: Hot Water Fixation Technique for Embryo Isolation

S. No.	Embryonic Developmental Stage	Temperature of Water (°C)	Dipping Duration (Minutes)
1.	24 hrs (1st day) (Stage 5)	70	3-4
2.	36 hrs (2nd day up to blastokinesis) (Stage 18)	75	4-5
3.	Blastokinesis to head pigmentation (Stage 22-27)	76	5
4.	Head pigmentation to blue egg stage (Stage 27-29)	77	6

(b) Potassium Hydroxide Technique (KOH)

- Prepare 2-4 per cent KOH solution.
- Boil the KOH solution up to boiling point (60°C).
- Dip the egg sheet or loose eggs in boiling KOH ((60°C) solution for 30 seconds.
- Care is to be taken that the embryos do not get dissolved in KOH solution.
- Transfer the content under tap water.
- Squirt water with force using dropper over eggs to release embryos.
- Transfer the released embryos carefully on to a micro-glass slide with the help of a dropper.
- Observe under microscope.
- Identify the stage of embryonic development.

(c) Transparent Technique

- Whole eggs are fixed in carmine for 30 minutes at 30°C.

- Transfer and preserve eggs then in 70 per cent alcohol.
- De-chorinised the eggs.
- Transfer the egg in 1 per cent HCl for 12 hrs at 50^{0}C.
- Embryo becomes visible.
- Stain with Borax carmine or Haematoxylin.

- *Permanent Slide Preparation*: Permanent slides for various developmental stages can be prepared for future reference. The embryos are isolated from egg shell adopting either hot water or KOH embryo isolation technique. The isolated embryos free from yolk are washed in distilled water. The washed embryos are passed through different grades of alcohol as indicated below (Table 4.7).

Table 4.7: Dehydration of Embryos for Staining

S. No.	Alcohol (%)	Dipping Duration (minutes)
1.	30	20
2.	50	10
3.	70	10

After washing the embryos in 70 per cent alcohol for 10 minutes, stain in Borax carmine for 5-20 minutes keeping in view of the intensity of colour required. After required colour is developed, embryos are washed again in 70 per cent alcohol for 2-3 minutes. The stained embryos are again passed through different grades of alcohol as indicated below (Table 4.8).

Table 4.8: Dehydration of Embryos for Mounting

S.No.	Alcohol (%)	Dipping Duration (minutes)
1.	80	10
2.	90	10
3.	Absolute	2-10

The embryos are again washed in absolute alcohol for 2-3 minutes and then passed through xylene for 1-2 minutes. The embryos are then mounted with DPX and covered with cover-slip avoiding air bubbles to enter the slide. The slide thus prepared is kept in an oven for 2-3 days maintained at 40^{0}C.

Suitable Embryonic Stages for Cold Preservation and Release

- Embryonic stages ideal for chilling is Stage 5 (24 hrs) to Stage 7 (48 hrs).
- Embryonic stage ideal for different hibernation schedule is Stage 8 (diapause stage).
- During cold storage, when diapause is in the stage of termination, the embryo reaches 10/11 stage depending on the duration of cold storage. When reaches Stage 11, it is fit for release and incubation.
- Embryonic developmental stages decide when long-term preservation of bivoltine eggs and double refrigeration can be undertaken. For this, when embryo reaches Stage 11 are released from cold storages and transferred at intermediate temperature (15^{0}C) for 3 days. During this period, the embryos reach Stage 15 which is suitable for re-refrigeration at 2.5^{0}C temperature for 10-40 days. The technique for prolonging the refrigeration is known as intermediate care. During intermediate care, if embryos reach Stage 16, instead of Stage 15, then they are not suitable for re-refrigeration or double refrigeration and such eggs can be incubated, brushed and reared. By adopting intermediate care, embryos retain its vitality and withstand long-term cold storage besides ensuring hatching in a single day. Embryonic Stage 5 at 10^{0}C and Stage 15 at 5^{0}C are suitable for long-term preservation of cross breed multivoltine eggs. However, cold storage of multivoltine eggs should be avoided as-far-as possible.

CHAPTER 5

Rearing of Chawki Silkworms

In temperate and sub-tropical climates, silkworm rearing is carried out twice in a year in spring and autumn season or three times in spring, summer and autumn coinciding with the growth and production of leaves (Kamili and Masoodi, 2004). However, in tropical regions, where mulberry growth is continuous throughout the year, silkworms are reared five to six times.

The rearing of young age silkworm up-to 2nd stage is known as chawki rearing. Failure of silkworm crops often traced to bad management and faulty rearing practices in-vogue to rear young age silkworm larvae. Young age silkworm rearing technique has undergone sea changes during the recent years based on principles of mulberry cultivation, silkworm larval growth, silkworm physiology and nutritional requirement (Rajan *et al.* 1996). The chawki larvae required ideal environmental conditions and quality tender mulberry leaves for robust and healthy growth and resistance to diseases and stress conditions at the later larval stages during development. Chawki rearing is a vital aspect in sericulture industry which determines development of healthy larvae and harvesting of successful cocoon crop. In India the conditions at farmers level is more heterogeneous with regard to rearing facilities, maintenance of optimum environmental conditions and cultivation practices and therefore, chawki rearing is must to reduce the crop loss and to increase the cocoon yield per unit area. Chawki rearing has many advantages *viz;*

- Ensuring uniform embryonic growth and good hatching.
- Minimizing the missing larvae and thus resulting in higher larval population.
- Robust, healthy and disease free growth of larvae.
- Prevention of crop loss and stabilization of cocoon crop.
- Minimizing the occurrence of outbreak of diseases by synchronizing the crop rearing.
- Improvement in quality of cocoon.
- Easy and effective crop monitoring.
- Increase in cocoon yield per unit area.
- Reduction is rearing expenditure.
- Effective utilisation of saved labour and time for other activities.

Silkworm layings should be procured only from the Silkworm Seed Production Centres (SSPCs) or Licensed Seed Producers (LSPs) which are tested and certified as Disease Free Layings (DFLs). The silkworm layings should be transported in transportation boxes during cooler hours of the day to avoid exposure of layings to extreme temperature and humidity. Under normal package of practices, 250-300 DFLs of silkworm can be reared from the leaves available from one acre of mulberry field. The silkworm eggs reaching to incubation centres/chawki rearing centres are preserved under optimum environmental conditions of temperature (25 $\pm$ 2^{0}C), RH (75 $\pm$ 5%) and photoperiod (16 L: 8 D) for healthy growth of larvae during embryonic development, so as to suit the silkworm eggs to develop normally to provide uniform and maximum hatchability on the expected day. The layings after procuring from the grainages are spread in a single layer on a paraffin paper spread in the rearing trays. Wet foam pads are placed around the layings and covered with another paraffin paper to provide ideal conditions of temperature and humidity. Two days before hatching, the color the eggs changes to lighter shade with blue pigmentation in the head region. This is the head pigmentation stage. On the next day, the egg color changes to almost blue/blackish and is called body pigmentation stage. These two stages are very sensitive to low humidity.

Black Boxing of Silkworm Eggs

Black boxing of silkworm is the technique subjecting the developing eggs to a totally dark condition, to synchronize the circadian rhythm of the silkworms. This ensures uniform synchronized hatching of eggs on a specific day within a short period. Black boxing should be done on the 8th or 9th day of incubation *i.e.,* on the onset of eye-spot or black head stage. The uniform hatching of all the eggs can be made possible when these eggs are exposed to light after specific period of black boxing. Black boxing is done by covering the silkworm eggs in black craft paper or black cloth. To avoid escape of newly hatched silkworm larvae from the egg sheet, the eggs must be wrapped in tissue paper during the body pigmentation stage. The cover is clipped and kept in the rearing tray surrounded with wet foam pad and covered with paraffin paper. On the day of hatching, at 7.00-8.00 AM, the covers are opened and layings exposed to mild light. Within 2 hours all the eggs will hatch. For acid treated bivoltine eggs a minimum of 60 hrs of black boxing and for hibernating eggs 72 hrs of black boxing is required. If hatching is to be postponed due to some unavoidable reason, then after one day of incubation, eggs can be preserved for 10 days at 5^0C. But if incubation period has passed for two days then the incubation is continued till the body pigmentation stage and then can be preserved at 5^0C for 3 days without having any deleterious effect on the development and physiology of silkworm eggs.

Brushing of Silkworm Eggs

The process of transferring the freshly hatched silkworm larvae to the rearing bed provided with mulberry leaves is known as brushing. The suitable time for brushing of newly hatched larvae is about 10 AM as most of the larvae hatch by 8.00-9.00 AM and develop good appetites within one to two hours of hatching. In order to obtain uniform hatching, developing eggs at blue stage are kept in black boxes 48 hrs prior to hatching day. On the day of hatching, in the morning, eggs are exposed to defused light, so that the larvae hatch uniformly in response to phototropic stimulus. By this method, more than 90 per cent hatching can be achieved in short period of one to two hours. Newly hatched larvae are black and hairy and look like black ants. At the time of brushing, the mulberry leaf is cut to fine ribbons and sprinkled over the hatched larvae to facilitate easy transfer of larvae from egg sheet to rearing bed. After half an hour, the worms are tapped on the rearing bed in the tray and 0.5 sq. cm., cut tender mulberry leaves are fed. The size of the bed for 25 DFLs should be 25 sq. cm. For brushing of silkworm larvae, soft camel brush or feather should be used to avoid damage to the newly hatched larvae.

Methods of Brushing

The method of brushing in practice is briefly described below–

(a) *Brushing of Eggs on Sheets:* On the day of hatching, the egg sheets are removed from the black boxing, wrapping tissue paper is opened and egg sheets are spread uniformly in one layer in the brushing tray. After one or two hours of exposure to light, when more than 90 per cent hatching is observed, the egg sheet with tray is removed from the light source and chopped tender mulberry leaves cut into small size (0.5 cm^2) are sprinkled over the egg sheet with hatched larvae. The hatched larvae within a short-period crawl onto the tender leaves and starts feeding. After 1-2 hours, the sheets are removed, the bed is uniformly prepared with chop sticks providing suitable spacing and first feeding of chopped mulberry leaves is given. The rearing bed is covered with paraffin paper to complete the operation of brushing. Sometimes, the freshly hatched larvae are brushed with a feather from the egg card directly on the rearing trays. This method is not recommended for brushing as it may cause injury to the freshly hatched larvae.

(b) *Brushing of Loose Eggs:* Loose eggs are available in egg cases of 50 DFLs and are approximately 20,000 eggs in each. Eggs transported in the loose egg boxes are transferred to incubation-cum-brushing frames (36 cm x 23 cm x 1.5 cm). The eggs are spread uniformly on the frames. The eggs are covered with tissue paper and incubation frames are piled-up in the incubation room wherein 16 hrs light, 8 hrs dark, 25^{0}C temperature and 80-85 per cent humidity are provided till the head pigmentation day/stage. Light intensity on egg surface to be above 10 Lux. When the eggs reach the head pigmentation stage, the loose eggs are removed from the egg boxes and spread on a tissue paper. Black boxing is carried out as per procedure for 48 hrs. The eggs are exposed to light after 48 hrs of black boxing to get more than 90 per cent hatching. On the day of stipulated hatching, at the time of exposure to light, two mosquito nets are spread over the loose eggs one over the other having 3 mm mesh. After hatching of eggs, tender leaves chopped into small size (0.5 cm^2) are spread over the net. When the larvae have crawled over the leaves, the first net is lifted and placed onto the rearing tray and larvae are brushed using a soft feather. The second net facilitates separation of hatched egg shells and the unfertilized eggs. After 1-2 hours, the bed is uniformly prepared with chop sticks providing suitable spacing and first feeding of chopped mulberry leaves is given. The rearing bed is covered with paraffin paper to complete the operation of brushing.

Eggs in loose forms are more advantageous than sheets egg and some of which are presented below –

- Supply of quality silkworm eggs with higher hatchability.
- Supply of uniform and assured quantity of eggs independent of breed/hybrid/season/region/source of its production.
- Facilitates elimination of unfertilized, dead, poor quality and defective eggs to ensure supply of only good quality eggs and hence resulting in increased hatchability, cocoon productivity and stable cocoon crop.
- The egg recovery in grainages could be substantially increased as the healthy laying with low fecundity is also collected.
- Surface sterilization of eggs can be accomplished more effectively and completely.
- As loose eggs are supplied in standard unit by weight, distribution is considered more perfect as each and every indenter have equal number of eggs for same quantity of DFLs. A unit number of 20,000 eggs are packed in each loose egg case which is considered equivalent to 50 DFLs on paper-card.
- Since there is uniformity in distribution of eggs, evaluation/comparison between different breeds/hybrids and seasons on the performance of economic characters are more accurate and scientific.
- Handling is easy and space required during egg laying by moth as well as during incubation is comparatively less.
- Acid treatment of bivoltine silkworm eggs (pure as well as hybrid), their preservation, incubation and transportation is easy and more convenient.
- Quality of eggs can be judged more accurately.

Inspite of all these advantages, the production and supply of loose eggs is still not very much popular in India at commercial level due to certain disadvantages like –

- Calculation of hatching percentage is not accurate and at the same time difficult and time consuming also.
- This method cannot be advocated for reproductive egg production level *i.e.*, for use at Basic Seed Farms (BSFs) or selected P1 seed rearers.
- Technique for separation of unfertilized eggs is still not very accurate and therefore some unfertilized eggs are packed in the egg boxes which affect hatching at commercial level.
- Loose egg production is more laborious, cumbersome and time consuming if performed in smaller quantities.
- Since the minimum unit handled in each case is 50 DFLs, farmers have to inevitably take the eggs in multiples of 50 DFLs irrespective of their rearing capacity, which sometimes leads shortage of leaf at the later stage of rearing leading to poor cocoon crop.
- Surface disinfections of eggs though carried out at the time of production but cannot be repeated at chawki rearing centres before incubation.
- Handling of loose eggs is cumbersome as differentiation of non-hibernating and hibernating eggs is difficult.

Time of Brushing of Larvae

Black boxed silkworm eggs are exposed to light in the morning at 6 AM and by 8 AM - 9 AM all those eggs that are expected to hatch complete their hatching. Those eggs that do not hatch in the morning of first day are covered with thin paper and kept in incubator. After one or two hours of hatching, the newly hatched larvae get an appetite and begin to crawl about. This is the time for brushing. If the larvae are not brushed at this stage, they will get tired, hungry, weak and susceptible to diseases later. If the season is warm and dry, it is safe to transfer them to the rearing beds a little earlier.

Determination of Brushing Date

Brushing date is determined on the basis of mulberry budding, availability of leaf and suitability of the season.

Incubation is initiated 10 to 12 days prior to the date of brushing. Generally, incubation period varies with silkworm breeds/hybrids, incubation methods adopted and stage of embryonic development. Normally, hibernated eggs take 11-14 days and non-hibernated eggs 10 to 12 days for hatching from initiation of incubation.

Determination of Rearing Scale

Rearing scale is determined on the basis of availability of manpower, mulberry leaf productivity, space of rearing house, rearing tools, facilities etc. As sericulture is subsidiary occupation, rearing scale is generally determined on the basis of availability of family labour and mulberry leaf but if it is large scale or an exclusive farming, rearing scheme is chalked out well in advance based on employment and other factors as well.

Harvesting of Leaf

For rearing young age silkworms, the best time for harvesting mulberry leaf is either early in the morning or in the evening. As different quality of leaf is required for different instars, a systematic leaf harvest is followed. During bright sunlight leaf plucking as far as possible should be avoided because in the daytime, a rise of air temperature causes evaporation from leaves and therefore harvested leaves are liable to wilting during storing. The mulberry garden should be set up near to the rearing place to avoid long transportation time, which makes leaves liable to wilting. If mulberry plantation is nearby, fresh leaves can be given to the silkworms. The harvested leaves should be packed loosely and transported rapidly to keep their freshness as much as possible.

Preservation of Fresh Leaves

The storage duration of fresh mulberry leaves should not be beyond 24 hours. The leaves must be stored at a place where the lowest evaporation takes place. The freshly harvested succulent leaves undergo rapid changes following harvest. The loss of moisture particularly is very rapid during hot dry seasons and this affects the palatability of leaves for silkworms. If temperature is high, leaves wither fast and thus become nutritively poorer. To prevent withering of leaves, attempts are made to maintain the relative humidity in the storage room to its required optimum level. Leaves are preserved loose under a wet gunny cloth which could be kept sufficiently wet all the time by sprinkling water on it repeatedly at convenient intervals. The larvae that are fed with such water treated leaves during preservation should be adequately spaced so that there may be proper ventilation in the rearing beds. Care should also be taken to see that directly wet leaves carrying water droplets over them are strictly avoided as this would lead to diseases. If any droplets are found on the leaves, they should be wiped out before being given for feeding to the silkworms.

In rainy season however, the situation exits quite opposite to that exits in summer. The humidity is generally high and hence problem is not of leaf moisture preservation but that of removing excess moisture present in the leaf. The leaves harvested in the rainy season should be spread out thinly on the floor to driven out excess moisture present on the surface of the leaf before feeding to the silkworms. Sprinkling of water for preservation of leaf is not necessary during this season.

Characteristics of Young Age Silkworm

The rearing of first two instars of silkworm form the young age raering. Third instar is also more or less close to young age rearing in its nutritional and environmental requirements. Therefore young age silkworm rearing refers growing of silkworm larvae up-to second or even third instar/moult. Some of the characteristics and requirement of young age silkworm is presented below –

(a) Young silkworms, particularly those in the first instar, have a high growth rate. During the first instar, body weight increases by 10-15 times, whereas in the other instars the weight increases by 5-6 times only. Similarly, per unit body weight the amount of food supplied, oxygen intake and evaporation are largest in the first instar.

(*b*) Young silkworms have stronger resistance against high temperature, high humidity and bad ventilation than grown silkworms. Therefore, rearing them slightly at high temperature and humidity results in higher silk productivity.

(*c*) Young silkworms are less resistant to pathogenic micro-organism than grown silkworms and therefore rearing of young silkworms requires more attention, care and hygienic conditions which has great impact on the stabilization of cocoon crop.

(*d*) Cool and low humid conditions are bad for the growth and development of young age silkworm larvae as these conditions harm the health of larvae and lead to poor cocoon quality with low productivity.

(*e*) Young silkworms are strong against dirty air but weak against carbonic acid gas, ammonia, muscardine etc. If the concentration of carbon dioxide gas in rearing room or in rearing box exceeds 2 per cent, the growth of silkworms is retarded. If temperature rises to 30^{0}C or higher, viral diseases may be liable to occur.

(*f*) In newly born larvae, water content is very low but increases rapidly up to second instars when feeding starts. Silkworm requires high water content in mulberry leaves to supply the needed water requirement in their body.

(*g*) Of the total requirement of leaf during the rearing period only 6.00 to 7.00 per cent is utilised during chawki rearing (up-to 3rd instar) but the larvae grows 400 times in body weight and 300 times in body size during this period. Therefore, maintenance and supply of good quality nutritive leaf supply is essential from brushing to 3rd stage rearing for success of silkworm crop and harvestation of stable cocoon crop with higher quantity.

(*h*) The growth rate of 1st instar larvae is very fast, and if nutrition is poor the growth will be retarded leading to poor cocoon crop.

Mulberry Leaves for Young Age Silkworm Rearing

It is desirable to provide mulberry leaves suited to various phases of growth during the young larval stage. Each age of silkworm larvae could conveniently be divided into seven stages *viz;* first feeding stage, sparse eating stage, moderate eating stage, active eating stage, pre-moulting stage, last feeding stage and moulting stage. Larvae have good appetite at the first feeding stage and comparatively little appetite at the sparse eating and moderate eating stage. They eat the most at the active eating stage. Therefore, quantity of leaf should be regulated according to the feeding patterns.

Mulberry leaves to be fed to young silkworms must have high moisture value. Feeding of leaves having a poor nutritive value reduces the resistance of young silkworms against diseases. The standard leaf positions suitable for rearing of various young stages of silkworms are –

- *Newly Hatched Larvae*: 3rd and 4th yellowish green leaves from the top.
- *First Instar*: 4th and 5th tender leaves from the tip below the leaves exposed to maximum light *i.e.*, top most full blown leaves which are light green.
- *Second Instar*: 5th to 7th leaves from the top turning to dark green.
- *Third Instar*: 7th and 8th leaves from the top, which are dark green in color.

The mulberry leaf suited as food to the silkworm must contain several chemical constituents' *viz;* water (80%), protein (27%), carbohydrate (11%), minerals and vitamins besides suitable physical features such as suitably tenderness, thickness, tightness etc., in order to be eaten by the silkworms. The nutrient composition in mulberry leaves differs according to the age. Younger the leaf, higher the protein content and lower the carbohydrate content (Table 5.1). The maximum light exposed leaves are those, which are yellow-green and have extremely shiny surface or luster. It is desirable to provide most suitable leaves close to the standard to the larvae but if these leaves differ in maturity to some extent, they can be mixed and provided. To obtain leaves suited for young silkworm rearing, it is advisable to establish a special mulberry field for young age silkworms rearing *i.e.*, chawki garden and to ensure its proper management.

Table 5.1: Nutrient Composition in Mulberry Leaves (%)

Position of Leaves from the Top	Water Content	Dry Matter	Protein	Composition of Dry Matter			
				Carbo-hydrates	Oil	Fiber	Ash
1	81.75	18.25	35.06	8.34	2.42	9.61	9.53
5	77.25	22.75	28.75	20.34	2.10	9.78	8.61
10	72.96	27.02	24.24	24.86	3.45	10.08	9.39
15	73.19	26.81	23.06	21.53	4.30	10.36	10.97
20	74.24	25.76	19.88	19.53	4.67	10.60	13.37
25	75.75	24.25	21.81	18.93	4.97	10.82	15.06

Rearing Environment

Climatic conditions including temperature, humidity, air circulation, gases and light affect the growth and development of silkworm resulting in influencing productivity and quality of silk, it is necessary to regulate maximum productivity of good quality cocoons. These factors, shows a significant interaction and their effect on the physiology of larvae vary depending upon combination of factors, developmental stage, nutritive status of feed etc.

(i) *Temperature:* Success of sericulture industries depends on various variables but environmental conditions such as biotic and abiotic factors are of particular importance. Among the abiotic factors, temperature plays a major role on growth and productivity of silkworm (Benchamin and Jolly, 1986). Since silkworms are cold-blooded animals, temperature has a direct effect on the growth, development and physiological activity, in nutrient absorption, digestion, blood circulation, respiration etc. Temperature has a direct correlation with the growth of silkworm and wide fluctuation in temperature is harmful for the development of silkworms. Rise in temperature increases various physiological functions and with a fall in temperature the physiological activities decreases. With the increase in temperature, the larval growth and development is accelerated resulting decrease in larval duration, while at low temperature growth and development is slow leading to prolong larval period. Generally the temperature range for normal growth is 18^{0}C-30^{0}C, but the optimum temperature range for rearing of young age larvae of bivoltine strain is 27^{0}C-28^{0}C for 1st and 2nd instars and 25^{0}C-26^{0}C for 3rd instar. In case of multivoltine strains slightly higher rearing temperature than that required for bivoltine is necessary. The room temperature is generally low during winter and high during summer months and therefore suitable measures should be adopted to regulate it to the optimum level. During winter, chawki rooms should be kept warm and particularly during night windows should be kept closed. In the day, as outside temperature goes up, the doors and windows should be opened to allow warm air in the room. During summer season, when day temperature is high, all the windows of chawki room should be kept open. Simultaneously, doors and windows are covered with wet gunny cloth during hot days to reduce the temperature and increase the humidity (Rahmatthulla, 1999). Otherwise suitable air cooler can be used for the purpose.

(ii) *Humidity:* Humidity also plays an important role in the chawki silkworm rearing. It has mostly indirect effect on growth and development. Humidity influences silkworm physiology indirectly through withering of leaves and sanitation of rearing beds. Under too dry conditions, the leaves wither very fast and become unsuitable for feed, resulting in retarded growth of larvae. Retarded growth of young age larvae makes them weak and easily susceptible to diseases and other adverse conditions. Under dry conditions, especially during winter and summer months, leaves wither very fast and consumption of leaf will be less. This affects growth of larvae and results in wastage of leaf in the rearing bed. Retarded growth of young silkworm larvae makes them weak and susceptible to diseases.

Ordinarily high relative humidity during rearing of young age silkworm larvae results in lesser loss of silkworm larvae than low relative humidity. During moult and throughout the moulting phase, the humidity should invariably be maintained slightly lower than in the rearing period. Humidity during rearing phase of 1st, 2nd and 3rd instar should be maintained at 85 per cent - 90 per cent, 85 per cent and 80 per cent respectively. If the air of the rearing room is too moist, it becomes favorable for growth of pathogenic microbes and consequently silkworm suffers from diseases. For regulating humidity in the rearing bed, paraffin paper and wet foam pads or paper bands are used. If humidity is too low, sprinkling of water on the floor may be found useful to increase it. As Chawki Rearing Centres (CRCs) are mostly maintained by Government agencies, humidifier with humidistat is used to regulate humidity in the rearing room.

(iii) Ventilation: Silkworms like any other animal requires fresh air for their various physiological activities. The freshness of air can be determined by its CO_2 contents. Due to respiration, carbonic acid gas is released in the rearing bed and rearing room. Although atmospheric CO_2 content is generally 0.03 per cent - 0.04 per cent in the rearing room but it can increase due to firewood, coal, smoke of fuel, carbon dioxide produced due to fermentation of leaves on rearing beds, respiration of mulberry leaves, carbon mono-oxide, ammonia and sulphur dioxide etc., and these gases are injurious to growth, development and health of silkworm larvae. When built up of these poisonous gases reaches beyond the tolerance limit of silkworm larvae, they start to show the symptoms of sluggishness and even stop to feed. Young silkworm

larvae are more susceptible to the poisonous gases and hence artificial circulation of air is extremely useful in bringing down the temperature and humidity besides removing the poisonous gases from the rearing room. Carbon dioxide content exceeding 1 per cent in rearing room is reported to be bad for silkworm and the relation between concentration of CO_2 in a rearing room and mortality of silkworm is linear.

(iv) *Light:* Light constantly influences the physiology of silkworm. Silkworms are photosensitive and generally have a tendency to crawl towards the dim light. Larvae of silkworm do not prefer either strong light or complete darkness but usually light phase in contrast to the dark phase activates the larvae preferring light within the range of 15-30 lux. Rearing in either complete darkness or in bright light leads to irregularity in growth and moulting. Light phase usually makes larval duration longer than the dark phase. Photo phase for rearing of silkworms should be 16 hours light per day followed by a Scot phase of 8 hours. It is advisable to rear silkworms in dim light during the daytime and in the dark during at night for healthy growth of larvae. Rearing of silkworms in continuous light delayed growth considerably leading to appearance of pentamoulters and reduced larval and cocoon weights.

Methods of Chawki Rearing

Different methods are in practice for rearing of early stages of silkworm. In all methods, importance is given to maintain optimum required temperature, humidity and photoperiod for vigorous and healthy growth of larvae. Mostly, three methods (Benchamin, 1992) are in practice for rearing of young silkworms. They are –

(a) Paraffin paper method.

(b) Box rearing method.

(c) Hot chamber rearing method.

(a) *Paraffin Paper Rearing Method:* This method is also known as covered rearing method. In this method, paraffin paper is used at the bottom as well as on the top of rearing trays to cover it. The objective of covering rearing trays with paraffin paper is to ensure optimum humidity in the bed and to keep mulberry leaves fresh for a longer period to ensure full nourishment and uniform development. Feeding is mostly given two to three times a day. The paraffin paper used for rearing of young silkworms should be of superior quality with melting point of above 55^{0}C. Superior quality paraffin paper could be used repeatedly which will result in lowering of rearing costs. Polythene sheets can also be used in place of paraffin paper. Polythene sheet should not be more than 400 gauge thickness and can be used several times after disinfection. Blue polythene sheet is recommended for the purpose as it has more cooling effect on the larvae compared to other colours.

During the first two instars, the rearing bed should be covered at both the top and the bottom, with the four sided wrapped. The top covering should be removed at moulting stage to dry rearing bed. Before covering the bed with paraffin paper at the top of rearing bed, wet foam pads on all four sides of rearing bed are placed to maintained required humidity. The top paraffin paper must be removed at least 20 minutes prior to feeding in order to provide adequate aeration and to dispel accumulated toxic gases. At the time of moulting, a thin film of lime powder sprinkled over the bed helps to keep the bed dry. But if humidity is high or in places which are humid, there is danger of muscardine and therefore a thin layer of muscardine powder may be spread over the bed to protect the silkworm against diseases at the time of hatching, at each moult and in middle of each stage.

(b) *Box Rearing Method:* The box rearing method is preferred when temperature and humidity are lower than the requirement. Boxes or trays made up of wood or plastic are used for box rearing. The boxes may be with lid or without lids. Silkworms are reared in the boxes with a cover in which wet foam pads are placed around the rearing bed to provide high humidity. The frequency of feeding is 2-3 times a day. The cover and foam pads should be removed 30 minutes before each feeding and also during moulting in order to regulate humidity. The trays are arranged in cris-cross manner for allowing the rearing bed to dry. While using this method care must be taken to disinfectant the silkworms by sprinkling anti-muscardine powder because due to high humidity in the rearing beds, the larvae are subject to muscardine disease. Wooden boxes of uniform size of 4′ × 3′ or 3′ × 2′ with 4" depth are used for this type of rearing. Normally, 5-8 boxes are piled one over the other for rearing.

(c) *Hot Chamber Rearing Method:* This method is widely adopted by Chinese sericulturists for young age silkworm rearing. This method is useful only when both temperature and humidity are very low. With this method, over 30 per cent labour and about 25 per cent - 35 per cent leaves could be saved. This method has the advantage in maintaining uniform temperature, moisture and freshness of leaves, high leaf utilisation ratio, less frequency of feeding, uniform and fast larval development. Owing to the high humidity and high temperature existing in it, the hot chamber should be thoroughly sterilized before rearing. Rearing is done inside the chamber in trays piled on chawki stand or on small rearing stand. Rearing is done by using paraffin paper as a seat and cover or by wrapping in paraffin paper. Chamber is also provided with ventilators so that aeration inside the chamber is achieved. A chamber with 6′ × 4′ × 5′ can accommodate 300 DFLs till second moult. Rearing is done as per standard procedure.

Nutrient Requirement for Chawki Larvae

- Chawki worms should be fed with succulent mulberry leaves rich in nutrients and moisture content *viz;* water content (80%), protein (27%) and carbohydrates (11%).

- Separate chawki garden with superior mulberry variety are maintained by providing irrigation and inputs such as FYM and chemical fertilizers in the recommended dose (FYM: 40 MT; N: P: K: 300:150:150).
- Select first glossy leaf from the top of branch for 1st feeding at the time of brushing and with the advancement in larval age the first 3-4 tender leaves can be used.
- Leaf harvest must be done in the morning and evening.
- Preserve the mulberry leaves in a cool place covered with wet gunny cloth.
- In dry season, sprinkle water over leaves and preserve them under wet gunny cloth.
- Chopped leaves should be fed to worms for uniform growth.
- Four feeding schedule *viz*; 6 AM, 10 AM, 4 PM and 10 PM should be followed.
- Stop feeding when above 90 per cent worms settle for moult and resume when 95 per cent worms comes out of moult.
- 30 minutes before feeding, the paraffin paper or polythene sheets covering the larvae are removed and after feeding the rearing beds are again covered with paraffin/ polythene sheets.
- The size of the leaf fed should be 0.50-1.00 cm^2 for 1st instar and 1.50-2.50 cm^2 for 2nd instar.
- Size of the leaf should be reduced when worms start settling for moult.

Spacing of Larvae During Chawki Rearing

To attain good survival, healthy growth of larvae and to harvest successful cocoon crop, optimum spacing of larvae in the rearing bed is essential. The larvae should be evenly distributed in the rearing bed, so that neither they are overcrowded nor over spaced. Over spacing leads to considerable wastage of chawki mulberry leaf while overcrowding in the rearing bed leads to insufficient consumption of leaf by the developing larvae, resulting in poor growth and higher incidence of diseases at the later stages of development. The larvae should be evenly distributed in the rearing bed, so that neither they are overcrowded nor over spaced. Recommended bed spacing can be provided and adjusted at the time of feeding taking into account of larval population per square feet as a guide. Spacing required for 100 DFLs of Bivoltine silkworm during chawki rearing is presented below (Table 5.2).

Table 5.2: Spacing for 100 DFLs Larvae of Bivoltine during Chawki Rearing

Larval Instar	Spacing Required (sq. ft.)		Larvae/sq. ft.	
	Beginning	At the End	Beginning	At the End
I	6.00	24.00	8300	2100
II	24.00	65.00	2100	800
III	65.00	150.00	800	350

If the larvae are overcrowded or over spaced in the rearing bed many problems may arise which may lead to poor cocoon crop at the time of harvest and therefore should be avoided.

Frequency of Cleaning

The silkworm settles for first molt after 3.0 t- 3.5 days from the day of brushing, if temperature, humidity and photoperiod are to the optimum level. When the symptoms of molting in larvae are observed, quantum of feed and size of leaf should be reduced. When larvae enter into molt, the paraffin paper/polythene sheet which are used for covering of larvae are removed and bed is allowed to dry up. The bed is spread and lime powder is dusted over the bed to dry it fast. Leaf over leaf and accumulated litter in the bed contributed to increase bed humidity and temperature besides causing multiplication of pathogens. Generally bed cleaning is not preferred in the 1st instar as it increases percentage of missing larvae but bed is spread sufficiently to free aeration and to dry up fast. First molt generally takes 20-24 hrs and therefore when larvae are out of molt, the bed disinfectant is dusted and after half an hour first feeding is given. Bed cleaning is performed after that only. Cleaning is carried out twice during 2nd instar, first after larvae are out of first molt and the second after larvae prepares to enter into second molt. In the 3rd instar also, two times bed cleaning is carried out, first after 2nd molt and second when larvae prepares to enter into molt. As young silkworms are very delicate, they should not be handled directly, instead nylon net of mesh size 1.00 Cm^2 is used for cleaning. Nylon/cleaning net are spread over covering the full bed. Feeding is given over the net. After some time or at the time of next feed when larvae crawl over the net, the net along with larvae is lifted and placed in another tray and fresh feeding is given by providing sufficient spacing and covered with paraffin paper.

Chopping of Leaves

While supplying mulberry leaves for feeding to young age silkworms, it is necessary to chop and provide them in the recommended sizes and quantities. While rearing the young age silkworms, the size of chopped leaves is increased as the larvae develop. The common size is 0.5 cm^2 - 1.0 cm^2 for the 1st instar, 1.5 cm^2 - 2.5 cm^2 for the 2nd instar and 3.0 cm^2 - 4.0 cm^2 for the 3rd instar. However, when the larvae are out of each moult, the first feeding is again given with slightly reduced size chopped leaves. Mulberry leaves are chopped with chopping knife on a thick wooden board. The wooden board is mostly 3 feet in length and 2 feet in width. However, in case of large scale rearing, the use of chopping machine is recommended. The amount of mulberry leaves to be given as feed to silkworm and the frequency of feeding etc., are variable according to the rearing temperature, humidity, ventilation, spacing and types of mulberry leaves etc.

However, at optimum temperature and humidity, the amount of mulberry leaves supplied to silkworms, frequency of feeding etc., for 10,000 are given in Table 5.3.

Table 5.3: Standard Chart for Chawki Silkworm Rearing (25 Dfls or 10,000 Larvae)

Factors	1st Instar	2nd Instar	3rd Instar
Temperature (^{0}C)	27-28	27-28	25-26
Humidity (%)			
Rearing	85-90	85	80
Moulting	75-80	75	75
Feeds per day (No.)	4	4	4
Quantity of leaf (kg)	1.50	4.00	16.25
Leaf size (cm^2)	0.50-1.00	1.50-2.50	3.0-4.0
Bed cleaning	1	2	2
Bed disinfectant (gm)	15	30	60
Larval period (days)	3.0-3.5	2.5-3.0	3.0-4.0
Moulting period (hrs)	20	20-24	20-24
Larvae/sq. ft.	2100	800	350

Care During Moult

The silkworm enters two times in moult during chawki rearing. Under optimum rearing conditions, the 1st instar larvae takes three to three and half days to settle for 1st moult and two to two and half days for 2nd moult. The moulting duration is approximately 20-24 hrs in 1st and 2nd instars at recommended temperature (27-28^{0}C) and humidity (85-90%). When the worms' starts settling for moulting, the top paraffin paper and wet foam pads are removed in order to provide low humidity. When all the larvae settle for moult, slaked lime is dusted @ 4-5 g/sq. ft. During moulting, the bed is spread to reduce its thickness and to allow the left over leaves and bed for drying. Feeding is resumed when more than 95 per cent of the larvae are out of moult. Before feeding the larvae, bed disinfectants (vijetha/ankush) @60 and 120 gm/ 100 DFLs in the first and 2nd instar are dusted over the larvae and feeding is provided half an hour later. As the mouth parts of freshly moulted larvae are delicate, it is advisable to give tender leaves. Give full feed when their appetite increases. Any mishandling and bad maintenance of environmental conditions during moulting period may lead to irregular moulting which will affect the larval health and ultimately quality of cocoon.

Larval Protection During Chawki Rearing

Unhygienic conditions of the rearing bed, rearing room and surroundings during chawki rearing are responsible for outbreak of various diseases at the later stages of development. If rearing room and appliances are disinfected properly before start of chawki rearing, the occurrence of pathogens are greatly reduced or even eliminated. However, in course of rearing, pathogens can be reintroduced in the rearing room through many other ways. Larvae pass out the pathogens along with litters, which can contaminate the mulberry leaf in the bed. If healthy larvae consume these contaminated leaves, there is possibility that the larvae will suffer from the disease. To avoid this, the rearing bed, rearing room and surroundings are to be dusted with recommended disinfectant.

(a) *Slaked Lime*: It is very widely used bed disinfectant and drying agent in sericulture. When it is dusted on the silkworm or left over leaves, it absorbs moisture and toxic gases in the rearing bed. When it absorbs moisture and become calcium hydroxide of pH more than 11, and when pathogen comes in contact with it, they will be inactivated and further secondary contamination will be reduced or eliminated. When lime is applied during moulting period, it dries the bed by absorbing moisture and toxic gases and releasing heat by its exothermic reaction with water molecules. The delicate skin of silkworm during the moulting period will be protected against pathogens by the lime. Further, lime also dries the left over leaves in the bed so that the leaves are not available for the early moulted silkworms, ensuring the

uniformity of larvae. Even the residual lime entering into the body of the silkworm through the leaf is not harmful to the silkworm. Hence the application of lime on the silkworm bed improves the micro-climate of the tray in additions to the inactivation of pathogens, which is a very important component in disease management. Lime should be applied 4-5 hrs after last feeding during each moult. There is no hard and fast rule regarding the quantity of lime to be used during moulting. However, a uniform film of dust of lime needs to be spread. Excess usage of lime is not harmful to silkworms.

(b) *Bed Disinfectant*: The bed disinfectant developed and recommended for use in sericulture during silkworm rearing is Resham Keet Oushad (RKO), Vijetha, Ankush, Suraksha, Sanjeevani, Resham Jyothi, Labex, Rakshak, Sericillin etc. Dusting of bed disinfectant helps in reducing the extent of contamination and spread of diseases during silkworm rearing. The method of application of bed disinfectant is as follows –

- Take the bed disinfectant powder on a thin muslin cloth/duster and dust it uniformly over the silkworm larvae in recommended quantity after bed cleaning.
- Bed disinfectants are to be dusted when larvae are out of moult but before feeding.
- It is to be dusted after moult once in 1st and 2nd instars.
- Do not dust when the larvae are in moult or when the silkworms are in eating stage.
- Feed silkworms after 30 minutes of dusting.
- The dusting should be uniform covering all the silkworms and rearing bed.

The schedule and recommended quantity of disinfectants to be dusted on silkworm is presented in Table 5.4.

Table 5.4: Standard Quantity of Bed Disinfectant Recommended for 00 DFLs during Chawki Rearing

Stage of Larvae	Vijetha/ Ankush (gm)	RKO (gm)	Resham Jyothi (gm)
Out of 1st moult (before resumption)	50	60	35
Out of 2nd moult (before resumption)	150	120	105
Total quantity (gm)	200	180	140

However, these bed disinfectants should be stored in air tight conditions, keep away from the reach of children, use exclusive cloth or the duster for the purpose of dusting and use mask to protect nose, eyes and ears during dusting.

Transportation of Chawki Larvae

Chawki larvae should be transported from the chawki rearing centres to the rearing site when they are in the 2nd moult or 2 feeds after the 2nd moult during cool hours particularly either in the early morning or late in the evening. The larvae mostly transported in rearing trays or crates designed for the purpose. Small vans are preferred for transportation of larvae from chawki rearing centres to the farmers rearing sites. However, transportation to long distances should be avoided. As soon as it reaches to the rearing site, the wax paper should be opened; larvae are spread in the tray kept on rearing stand for the rearing of the larvae.

Pests of Chawki Larvae

Among several factors, which influence the cocoon yield of silkworm seed as well as commercial cocoon production, silkworm diseases and the insect and non-insect pests form an important component. The mulberry silkworm is attacked by insects such as tachinid parasitoids, dermestid beetles, ants, earwigs etc., (Narayanaswamy and Devaiah, 1999). The pests and parasites other than insects are mites, nematodes, wall-lizards, rats, squirrels and birds that are also known to inflict considerable damage to silkworm and its crops (Khan *et al.* 2011). Ecologically, highly adoptive omnipresent rat and ants cause extensive damage to chawki silkworm larvae in the rearing rooms. Ten species of ants are reported associated with sericulture throughout the years in varying intensities. The ants established nests around the rearing establishments, gained entry through doors, windows and air outlets. Their activity is high during cooler hours of the day. If uncared, they can cause considerable loss to chawki silkworm larvae (Reddy *et al.* 1995; Harikrishna and Reddy, 1997). To protect silkworm larvae from the damage caused by ants, it is recommended that the rearing stand legs should always be placed in the centre of the ant well to avoid crawling of ants on the rearing stand. Also lower portion of the rearing stand is to be pasted with grease so that if any ant passes through the ant well should not go beyond certain point on the rearing stand and stuck on the grease. Further, bleaching powder and lime mixture dust should be dusted in and around the chawki room not only to maintain hygiene but also to stop crawling of minute individuals in the rearing establishment. To avoid entry of lizards and rats in the rearing establishments, it is recommended to have wire mesh on the windows and doors.

CHAPTER 6

Rearing of Late Age Silkworms

The rearing of grown up silkworms is known as late age rearing. The method of rearing of advanced stage larvae is different from that of young silkworms. Unlike the young silkworm larvae, the advanced stage larvae withstand high temperature and humidity. They normally thrive well under comparatively lower temperature and humidity than those for young larvae. The growth of advanced stage larvae is fast and the consumption of mulberry leaf is very high. The temperature should be around 24-25^{0}C during 4th instars and between 23-24^{0}C during 5th instars. Since the environmental conditions vary with the rearing season, suitable modification in the rearing method is necessary. For example, under high humidity conditions as in rainy season, more ventilation and greater spacing should be resorted to, and all care should be taken to avoid overfeeding to the larvae. During winter season, the rearing room should be warmed by some means to the optimum level. However, during summer and autumn season rearing, it is necessary to bring down the temperature and if there is high humidity, arrangement should be made to maintain it to the required level. Larvae should be provided with sufficient quantity of mulberry leaf during this active feeding stage. For late age silkworms, more mature leaves, which contain less of moisture and more protein content, should be used. Attention should be focused on proper preservation of leaf, as health of larvae depends very much on the quality and quantity of leaf consumed. If leaf is not sufficiently fresh, its edible quantity is reduced and worms tend to undergo starvation inspite of the presence of leaf in the rearing bed. It is advisable to give fairly a large quantity of leaf as feed during night. Rearing of 5th instars larvae needs more labour and attention to harvest good quality of cocoons. Labour requirement during late age rearing, especially during 5th instars is about 50 per cent of the total mandays requirement.

Characteristics of Grown Silkworms

Grown silkworm differs from young silkworms in many aspects –

(a) Grown silkworms are weak to high temperature, high humidity, poor ventilation and other metrological environments.

(b) The digested and ingested amount of mulberry leaves increases and they eat even over mature and somewhat less water content leaves. However, their digestion ratios are lower than those for young silkworms.

(c) They are resistant to poor quality of leaves, deficiency in feeding quantity, and other nutritional deficiencies.

(d) Their resistance to chemical is strong. Because of their characteristics, the environment and rearing techniques applicable to 4th and 5th instars differ greatly from those of young silkworms.

Rearing Environment

Temperature

Mulberry silkworms are poikilothermic (cold blooded) and therefore do not withstand the fluctuating tropical climates. However, they have primitive mechanism by which they regulate body temperature according to the surrounding temperatures. If the temperature of the surroundings increases, the physiological activities *viz;* ingestion, digestion, excretion, blood circulation, respiration, absorption etc., also increases considerably, this causes harm to the developing silkworms. The growth of silkworms will be delayed if the temperature and humidity are too low and accelerated if it is high leading to poor cocoon crop. The effect of ecological factors on larval duration and environmental adjustment in sericulture is studied by many workers (Patil and Gowda, 1986; Pandey *et al.* 2006) and stated that it is important to keep optimum rearing temperature and humidity for normal growth and development. The optimum requirement of temperature during later instars of larvae is presented in Table 6.1.

Table 6.1: Optimum Requirement of Temperature and Humidity

Instars	Temperature (^{0}C)	Humidity (%)
III	24-26	80
IV	24-25	75
V	23-24	70

However, it will be difficult for the farmers to maintain the optimum requirement of temperature for different larval stages, but efforts should be made that the temperature should not fall below 20^{0}C or exceeds above 30^{0}C. This is because the normal development of silkworm takes place between 20-30^{0}C temperature. Best result however, can be achieved if the temperature is maintained to the required optimum level. Wide fluctuation of temperature is very harmful to the developing silkworm larvae and should be avoided. Generally, the temperature is low during winter and rainy season and needs to be regulated with heating devices. Doors and windows should be closed during night. In the day time when temperature increases outside, the doors and windows should be opened to allow warm air in the rearing room. During summer, when day temperature is high, all the windows should be opened and simultaneously doors and windows should be covered with wet gunny cloths to reduce the temperature and increase the humidity. Otherwise suitable air cooler can also be used for the purpose. Intensive and careful domestication over centuries has apparently deprived silkworms of opportunity to acquire thermo-tolerance. Among many factors responsible for poor performance of Bivoltine strains under tropical conditions, the main culprit is the temperature (Rahmathulla, 2012).

Humidity

Humidity also plays very important role in the development of later instars of larvae and harvestation of good quality of cocoon. Body temperature, blood circulation and respiration rate in silkworm increases if humidity is high. Also, the water evaporation from the body of the silkworm reduces, weakening the resistance of larvae to diseases. Fungal diseases occurrence is high if the humidity in the rearing bed is high. Humidity requirement for the feeding period is different from that of the molting period. Comparatively low humidity is required during the period when larvae are in molt. Humidity directly affects the physiology activities of developing silkworms and indirectly the driage of mulberry leaves in the bed. At 90* or above humidity, if temperature is maintained at 26^{0}C-29^{0}C, they will grow without being much affected. The spinning and pupation period is longer in higher humidity conditions. However, if humidity is high, water evaporation in the boy of the silkworm will be restricted and resistance of larvae to diseases decreases. When humidity is low, the leaf withers very fast and this reduces leaf intake by the developing silkworm larvae resulting weak larvae and small cocoon. Recommended humidity for 3rd, 4th and 5th instars are 80 per cent, 75 per cent and 70 per cent respectively and efforts should be made to maintain this optimum humidity during rearing period to harvest good quality of cocoons.

Air Current

Air flow in the rearing house plays an important role and has tremendous effect on the silkworm rearing and stable cocoon crop. The 4th and 5th instars larvae consume about 90 per cent of the total requirement of leaf and accordingly also releases large quantity of water, which increases humidity in the rearing room. The rearing house also gets polluted with many types of gases *viz;* ammonia, sulphur dioxide, carbon dioxide, formalin fumes etc., through silkworm expiration, workers breath, mulberry leaves, fermentation of litter, burning of charcoal while increasing temperature etc. Excessive accumulation of these leads to death of larvae. Therefore, rearing rooms should have enough fresh air to avoid accumulation of these harmful gases. This can be achievement only when rearing room is well cross-ventilated. Carbon dioxide should not exceed above 1 per cent in the rearing house which is injurious to the health of larvae. The air current of 1.0 m/sec during 5th stage rearing reduces the larval mortality and improves ingestion, digestibility, larval weight, and cocoon weight and pupation rate compared to those recorded under zero ventilation conditions (Rajan and Himantharaj, 2005). The recommended air current during late age silkworm rearing is 1.7 m/sec during rearing period.

Light

Silkworms are photosensitive and prefer dim light (15-30 lux). They avoid strong light as well as darkness. In order to have uniform growth of larvae, direct light or one sided light in the rearing room should be avoided. Larvae of silkworm do not prefer either strong light or complete darkness but usually light phase, in contrast to dark phase, activates the larvae. If silkworms are fed in complete darkness during the life cycle, their larval duration is longer and cocoon quality becomes poor (Patil and Gowda, 1986). A simple way to find out that whether the light is sufficient in the rearing room is by holding a paper with some writing on it below the light and if one is able is see the writing but not necessarily to read the passage, then that light is sufficient for silkworm during day time. Mathur *et al.* (1995) studied the effect of photoperiod on rearing and stated that late age silkworm shows optimum growth at 16 hrs light and 8 hrs darkness during rearing period. Requirement of suitable temperature, humidity, air current and photoperiod during rearing of different larval instars are described in detail (Rapusas and Gabriel, 1976; Vijayakumari *et al.* 2001).

Areas of High Temperature and Low Humidity

- Avoid rearing house with asbestos or tin roof.
- Raise shade trees around the rearing house, cover the roof with coconut thatches, grass or palm leaves.
- Apply 'Cool Guard' to the roof top.
- Feed mulberry leaves with higher moisture content. Harvest mulberry leaves during cooler hours, sprinkle water and preserve them in dark and cooler area.
- Keep windward windows and floor level ventilators closed during hot period of the day.
- Provide wet gunny cloth curtain to the windows and doors.
- Wipe floor with water during day time once at 11 AM and again at 3 PM.
- Increase the frequency of feeding from 2-3 to 3-4 times a day.
- Feed reduced quantity of leaves during noon and more during night.
- During hot period, cover the bed with old newspaper, after feeding.

Areas of Low Temperature and High Humidity

- Regulate air circulation without causing suffocation.
- Use heaters (electrical or charcoal) to raise room temperature.
- Dust dry slaked lime powder on the rearing room floor.
- Dust dry slaked lime powder on the silkworms, after bed cleaning or before feeding in the morning.
- Avoid over feeding. Feed only the quantum of mulberry leaves, the larvae consumes during the feed period.
- Avoid accumulation of silkworm waste and faeces in the bed.

- Feed comparatively more mature leaves than the leaves fed during normal period.

Areas of Low Temperature and Low Humidity

- The rearing house will have to be heated artificially.
- Proper ventilation through windows must be provided.
- It is useful to place a metal container filled with water over the heater or stove to raise both temperature and humidity to the desired level.

Areas of High Temperature and Dryness

- Open the doors and windows of the rearing rooms and hang a moist cloth to provide humid air circulation in the room.
- Sprinkle water on the floor of the rearing room. Spraying of water on the roof reduces temperature and increases humidity.
- If daytime temperature is too high, doors and windows should be closed.
- Electric fan should be used to ventilate the room as and when required.
- In the evening doors and windows should be opened to allow cool air to circulate.

Areas of High Temperature and Humidity

- To protect the rearing house from direct sunlight, trees should be planted around the shed of rearing house.
- Good circulation of air will help to reduce the temperature to a considerable extent.

Planning for Rearing

Rearing Equipments

Following are the appliances required for rearing various stages of silkworm (Table 6.2). Their number varies depending on the silkworm breeds and number of DFLs reared. Therefore proper assessment of requirement is to be made before starting the silkworm rearing.

Table 6.2: Rearing Equipments Required for Silkworm Rearing

S. No.	Rearing Equipments
1	2
1.	Rearing house with verandah and shoot/leaf store room
2.	Mountages (for spinning)
3.	Sprayer with mask
4.	Room heater
5.	Humidifier
6.	Plastic bucket
7.	Rearing stand
8.	Rearing trays (plastic)
9.	Feeding stands
10.	Leaf chopping board
11.	Leaf chopping knives
12.	Leaf preservation chamber
13.	Ant well (to prevent crawling of ants into trays)
14.	Chapels
15.	Bed cleaning nets (different mesh sizes)
16.	Old news paper
17.	Foam pad (to maintain required humidity)
18.	Litter basket/vinyl sheet
19.	Plastic basins
20.	Leaf collecting basket
21.	Shoot rearing rack
22.	Chandrike/mountages
23.	Wash basin stand
24.	Foot cleaning mat
25.	Chop sticks (6" length)
26.	Feather

Contd...

1	2
27.	Paraffin paper/blue polythene sheet
28.	Muslin cloth (2 meter)
29.	Bed disinfectant
30.	Room disinfectant
31.	Lime and Bleaching
32.	Electronic balance
33.	Gunny cloth
34.	Mat (for collecting leaf after chopping)

(a) *Rearing House:* A rearing house of convenient size for self-rearing as well as for shoot rearing with a ledge all around to prevent rats from entering the building, having verandah all around with windows and doors to provide good ventilation and light is necessary.

(b) *Mountages:* Mountages are used to support the silkworm to spin cocoons.

(c) *Rearing Stand:* Rearing stands are made of wood or bamboo or iron rods. They should be light in weight to move them from one place to another. A rearing stand should be 7.5′ in height, 4.5′ in length and 3′ wide and should have 10 shelves with a space of 20cm between each shelf. The trays are arranged on the shelves.

(d) *Feeding Stand*: These are made of wood or iron with 2.7′ height for holding the trays during feeding to silkworms or cleaning..

(e) *Rearing Trays*: These are used to rear various stages of the silkworm and are usually made of bamboo or plastic so that they are light in weight for handing during silkworm rearing. Bamboo trays are either round with a diameter of 3.5′ to 4.5′ and a depth of 7.5 mm or rectangular measuring 2′ - 3′ × 3′ - 3.5′. The plastic trays are usually 2′ × 3′ size with a depth of 5 mm.

(f) *Ant Well*: Ant wells are provided to stop crawling of ants onto the trays and attacking the silkworms. They are made of stone blocks or aluminum. Each leg of rearing stand rests on the centre of the ant well and water is poured into the groove (2.5 cm) to stops the ants to crawl and reach to silkworms in the trays.

(g) *Paraffin Paper*: This is thick craft paper with paraffin wax with melting point of above 55^{0}C. It is used on the base and for covering the early stage silkworm to maintain proper humidity in the rearing bed and also to avoid withering of chopped leaves.

(h) *Chop Sticks*: These are usually made of bamboo or mulberry twigs measuring approximately 17.5 to 20 cm in length. These are tapering at one end. Direct handing of silkworms should be avoided for maintenance of proper hygienic conditions. Chop sticks are used to spread the bed and also to pick the diseases silkworm larvae.

(i) *Foam Pad Strips*: Long foam rubber strips of 2.5 cm wide and 2.5 cm thick of approximately size of the tray dipped in water are kept all around the silkworm rearing bed during rearing of chawki silkworm larvae to maintain optimum required humidity. As a substitute, newspaper folded into convenient size dipped in water can be placed around the bed.

(j) *Feathers:* Birds feather, preferably white are used for brushing the delicate silkworm larvae in to the rearing bed. They are also used to prepare the bed of required size.

(k) *Leaf Chopping Board:* This is made of soft wood and is used for cutting the leaf to the suitable sizes for feeding to different stages of the silkworm as per their requirement. The size of the chopping board is usually 3′ × 3′ 5 cm thick or may be of any other convenient size.

(l) *Leaf Chopping Knife:* Chopping knife is used for cutting the mulberry leaf of required size for feeding to different stages of the silkworm.. They are usually 1′ in length with a broad knife blade and wooden handle.

(*m*) *Leaf Preservation Chamber:* Mulberry leaves are harvested from the field and transported to rearing establishments for feeding to different stages of silkworms. They are preserved in cool rooms or in a room in heaps covered with wet cloths or polythene sheets to make it fresh and to avoid its withering. They can also be stored in leaf chamber of convenient size (3' × 5' × 3'). The chamber is covered with gunny cloth which is kept wet. During summer months and dry days, these gunny cloths are kept wet to avoid withering of leaf inside the chamber.

(*n*) *Bed Cleaning Nets:* These are made of cotton thread or nylon, woven into nets of different meshes to suit to size variations of different instars of silkworm larvae. They are used for cleaning the rearing beds.

Mulberry Leaf

Mulberry leaf is the sole food for rearing of silkworm and its quality exerts very important influence upon cocoon yield. The major constituents of the mulberry leaf are water and dry matter. The dry matter consists of proteins, carbohydrates, fats, inorganic salts and vitamins. All these chemicals are essential nutrients for physiological function and healthy growth of silkworm larvae. All these elements vary according to the position of leaves on the shoots, maturity of mulberry garden, time of harvest, conditions of storage of leaf, soil fertility, soil texture, variety of mulberry and weather conditions.

Quality and suitability of leaf has direct effect on the production of cocoon, quality of cocoons and silk and therefore effort should be made to select and feed most suitable leaf to feed the silkworm as per requirement according to their stage and age of development. Leaf assessment is to be done before starting the rearing. 100 DFLs silkworm larvae consume approximately 1250 to 1400 kg leaf from 3rd stage to spinning stage and accordingly after assessment of leaf availability, larvae are to be supplied to farmers for rearing. Otherwise, is more larvae are supplied for rearing, at the fag-end of rearing when larvae will be in vigorous stage of feeding, there will be shortage of leaf and larvae will become weak leading to poor cocoon crop. Leaf should be fresh for feeding. Wither leaf should not be fed to larvae as it leads to reduction in consumption of leaf and results in poor cocoon crop.

Selection of Mulberry Leaf

Quality and suitability of mulberry leaf has have a direct effect on cocoon yield, quality of cocoon and silk and therefore efforts should be taken to choose best quality of leaf to meet the requirement of different stages of developing silkworm larvae. Too tender or too matured leaves are not fit for feeding to late instar larvae. For late age silkworms, leaf harvest is done either by plucking leaf from the bottom which are dark green and mature, slow to wilt, rich in protein with moderate moisture content or by branch feeding which is also known as shoot rearing. In case of leaf feeding, whole leaf is given as feed without chopping and in branch feeding method, shoot is cut into convenient length to accommodate them in rearing racks. The shoot should be 7-8 weeks old after pruning. Leaf which is yellow, muddy, dusty or suffering from any kind of diseases should not be given as feed to silkworm. These types of leaf must be removed.

Leaf Preservation

Leaf preservation is an important step in tropical sericulture. It is better to supply fresh mulberry leaves to the developing larvae. However, considering the economics of labour and periodic deterioration of weather conditions, it is necessary to harvest and store enough quantity of mulberry leaf, which can be utilised subsequently for feeding. However, if the conditions during the preservation of mulberry leaf are not proper, the quality of leaf will deteriorate resulting in unstable cocoon crop.

During winter and spring season, the prevailing temperature and humidity conditions and normal moisture content of leaf mostly do not call for special method of leaf preservation because temperature is cool and humidity is high but at the same time, it is advisable not to preserve the mulberry leaf for a very long period. During rainy season, however, water content in the mulberry leaf is very high and if the same is supplied for feeding, it may lead to spread of various diseases. Therefore, the plucked leaves are first spread on the floor for some time (3-6 hrs) and then preserved in leaf chambers or under slightly wetted cloth or gunny.

During summer season, when the temperature is high and humidity is low, withering of leaf takes place very fast. To prevent withering of leaves, attempts are often made to increase and maintain humidity of the rearing room as well as of leaf preservation room. For this purpose, freshly harvested leaves are preserved in leaf chambers of any convenient size (3' x 5' x 3') lined with gunny cloth and covered with slightly wetted gunny cloth. In case of shoot harvest, they are made to stand erect on the floor and covered with wet cloth or gunny. In summer season, the cloth or gunny cover should be sprinkled or sprayed with water to keep them wet all the time.

Mulberry storage room should be clean and completely disinfected. Significance of such type of leaf preservation leads to gain in weight and good health of larvae resulting in stable cocoon crop. In order to save the mulberry leaves from wilting during storage, they are periodically shuffled. When mulberry shoots are stored, they are tied into loose bundles and kept erect/vertically on the floor. Shoots are harvested from the mulberry stumps with secateurs. Shoots should be harvested in the morning hours as this will keep them fresh and food value will be intact with enough water. Shoots harvested in the afternoon will have lost much water due to transpiration and their leaves will wither very quickly. However, it is advisable as a general practice to pluck or harvest leaf twice in the day, once in the morning and again in the evening during the cooler hours. First harvest of morning leaf should be given for 2nd and 3rd feeding of the day and 2nd harvest of evening should be given as night feed and also the next day morning feed. Sengupta *et al.* (1971) studied the effect of time of harvest of mulberry leaf on cocoon crop and quality and stated that harvesting of leaf should be monitored as per requirement. Heaping of leaf or shoots should be avoided as this will lead to fermentation and making leaf unsuitable for feeding to silkworm. Relative moisture loss from leaves of some mulberry varieties during storage/preservation (Govindan *et al.* 1988) and its influence on growth and silk production (Shivakumaraswamy *et al.* 2004; Rahmathaulla *et al.* 2006) is studied in detail and states that proper preservation of mulberry leaf after harvest is to be ensured to harvest stable cocoon crop with better productivity.

Method of Late Age Silkworms Rearing

For rearing the advanced age silkworm larvae, three methods of rearing are commonly in use. They are –

(a) Shelf/Tray rearing method.

(b) Shoot rearing method.

(c) Floor rearing method.

(a) *Shelf Rearing Method:* Rearing of silkworms in rearing trays arranged one over the other in tiers on rearing stand is called shelf rearing. Generally, rearing stands are arranged in rows parallel to the wall with adequate space in the centre for removing the trays and attending the cleaning of rearing beds and feeding to the silkworms. The trays are pulled out to provide the feed and then kept back. Each rearing stand can accommodate 14-16 rearing trays. This method has been followed for a very long time and in terms of optimum use of available space, it is very profitable and economical. In India, generally in West Bengal, sericulture farmers' use round bamboo trays of 1.2-1.4 meter in diameter for rearing of late age silkworms. Under this system of rearing, mulberry leaves are plucked individually and fed to the silkworms. Usually 4 feedings are given in a day and nets are used to clean the bed once in a day. Mostly for cleaning, it is advisable to spread the cleaning net in the tray before feeding in the morning. Leaves are broadcasted over the

net and larvae from below the net crawl on it. After, 3-4 hours, when almost all the larvae crawl on the leaf from below the net, it is removed and the refuse below the net are rejected and disposed off in pit made for the purpose. The net along with the larvae is again spread over the cleaned tray. Nets are left below the bed which will help in removing the removing the bed refuses while doing next cleaning. After the cleaning bed disinfectant should be dusted over the rearing bed to check the spread of contamination if any. Shelf rearing has the advantage of accommodating more silkworm larvae in a limited area than any other method.

(b) *Shoot Rearing Method:* In this method, the silkworms are reared on big branches in one or two tiers. The shoots are harvested from the fields and are fed to the silkworms straight away. The mulberry shoot rearing method is of various types *viz;* flat surface, slop, mixed, vertical slop, Fuji-type, Kamaboko type etc. Out of these methods, flat surface method is most popular in India. The rearing sheets are usually one meter wide and have any convenient length accommodating to the length of rearing house. In shoot rearing method, the number of feeds provided to the silkworms is 2 or 3 per day. The mulberry leaves should be uniformly distributed on the rearing bed so that each and every larva has equal access to the leaves. For this, the branches should not be too much bend, leaves should not be too dense and also the size of leaves should be medium.

As whole shoots are supplied for every feed, larvae kept moving upwards consuming the mulberry leaves. In this method, there is better aeration and therefore, it is possible to have 50 per cent more larvae per unit area of rearing sheet as compared to shelf or floor rearing method. Bed cleaning is performed once in 4th instars and also only once in 5th instars. During 4th instars, the rearing bed is often covered with plastic sheet in order to prevent excessive wilting of mulberry leaves. Just prior to ripening of larvae, they should be provided with whole leaves instead of shoots as otherwise; it will have an adverse effect on their subsequent rearing as well as mounting on cocoon frames. When the larvae are in moulting phase, the rearing bed should be kept dry by spreading lime or brunt husk over it.

To clean the bed, ropes of convenient lengths are spread parallel to each other lengthwise on the bed and after 2 or 3 feeds, when all the worms have crawled on the new branches; the bed held by ropes is rolled into loose bundles. After cleaning the beds, the rolled up branches and worms are transferred back on to the rearing beds and spread out again. The shoot rearing saves on labour cost up to 50 per cent compared to leaf feeding method, which constitute a major expenditure in silkworm rearing at the 4th and 5th instars. The amount of leaves required is reduced approximately by 25 per cent in 4th instars and 10 per cent in 5th instars. Worms and leaves do not come in contact with litter, hence chances of secondary contamination is also reduced. This method ensures better aeration in the bed with better cocoon and survival of larvae resulting in better harvest of cocoon in higher quantity. For rearing 100 DFLs a rearing house having a floor area of 400 sq. ft., is required for conducting rearing. As handling of silkworm is minimized, better hygienic conditions can be maintained which reduces chances of contamination and spreading of disease. The shoot rearing method for late age silkworms is described in detail by Sekharappa *et al.* 1993.

Advantages of Conducting Shoot Rearing is –

- Labour saving upto 50 per cent.
- Leaf saving upto 15 per cent,
- Reduced leaf driage in rearing bed.
- Bed area requirement of rearing of 100 DFLs is 15-20 per cent less.
- Handing of larvae during rearing is minimum. Larvae and leaves do not come in contact with litter and therefore chances of secondary contamination and spread of disease if any is reduced.

- Better aeration in the rearing bed to ensure better and uniform growth of larvae.
- Cocoon characteristics and effective rate of rearing (survival) is comparatively better.

(c) *Floor Rearing Method:* The floor rearing of silkworm is carried out on fixed rearing seats. The rearing seats arranged in 2 or 3 tiers as in shoot rearing method to accommodate as many silkworm larvae as possible. The rearing seat measures 1.0-1.5 meter in width and 5-7 meter in length or according to the convenient length of the rearing house. There should be sufficient space between two tiers to provide feeding to the larvae and for cleaning to the bed. This space is mostly kept in between 0.6-0.8 meter. The rearing seat is usually made of wood or bamboo strips. The larvae are fed with the leaves or branches cut into small pieces of 15 cm. The number of feeds provided per day is three or four. Bed cleaning is carried out with the help of rearing/cleaning nets in the same way as in the case of shelf rearing. Moreover, the bed cleaning is less frequent in floor rearing in comparison to shelf rearing. Bed cleaning is carried out twice during 4th instars and 3 times during 5th instars. During 4th instars, the rearing bed is covered with plastic sheet/wax paper to save mulberry leaves from drying. If there is too much humidity, the wax paper is removed. In order to reduce humidity in the rearing bed, lime powder is spread on it. The main difference in shelf rearing and floor rearing is that of labour requirement. In shelf rearing for pull out the rearing trays and again to put it on the rearing stand after every feeding and bed cleaning is saved in floor rearing method. Therefore, floor rearing is less laborious and less labour consuming in comparison to shelf rearing method. Economic characters of mulberry silkworm in relation to different rearing methods are studied and described in detail (Sharma, 1992; Kumaresan *et al.* 1999).

Bed Spacing

As silkworm grows from hatching to spinning by 10,000 times in weight, therefore sufficient spacing should be provided in the rearing bed during different developmental stages. The larvae should be evenly distributed in the rearing bed, so that neither they are overcrowded nor over spaced. Over spacing leads to considerable wastage of mulberry leaf and higher leaf cocoon ratio while overcrowding in the rearing bed leads to insufficient consumption of leaf by the developing larvae, resulting in poor growth and higher incidence of diseases and harvest of inferior quality of cocoon. Recommended bed spacing can be provided and adjusted at the time of feeding taking into account of larval population per square feet as a guide both for leaf feeding and shoot feeding larvae (Table 6.3 and 6.4). Spacing is done usually when the beds are cleaned. It is also necessary to provide wider spacing when temperature and humidity are higher than the optimum. Wider spacing enables free circulation of air and ensures reduction in temperature and humidity in the rearing bed. Comparative performance of various economic traits of silkworm reared under recommended spacing of Japanese, Chinese and Indian (Singh, 2001) indicates that Indian spacing is best to harvest stable cocoon crop with better qualitative and quantitative parameters. The influence of rearing space on growth, fecundity and hatchability is also studied by Roychoudhury *et al.* (1991) who recommended that proper spacing in the rearing bed should be provided for better growth and productivity.

Table 6.3: Spacing for 100 DFLs Larvae of Bivoltine during Late age Rearing (Leaf Feeding)

Larval Instars	Spacing Required (sq. ft.)		Larvae/ (sq. ft.)	Quantity of Mulberry Leaf (kg.)
	Beginning	At the End		
III	65.00	150.00	350	65.00
IV	150.00	300.00	160	195.00
V	300.00	600.00	80	1120.00

Table 6.4: Spacing for 100 DFLs Larvae of Bivoltine during Late Age Rearing (Shoot Feeding)

Larval Instars	Spacing Required (sq. ft.)		Quantity of Mulberry (kg.)
	Beginning	At the End	
III	65.00	150.00	138.00
IV	150.00	350.00	398.00
V	350.00	700.00	2240.00

If the larvae are overcrowded or over spaced in the bed many problems may arise which may lead to poor cocoon crop and therefore should be avoided. Some of these are –

- Poorly fed silkworm larvae.
- Uneven growth of larvae resulting into uneven moulting and varied sizes of cocoons.
- Crop losses due to outbreak of diseases precipitated by the weakness of underfed larvae.
- Irregular moulting leading to formation of two batches within the same population which will spin on different days. This will automatically increase moulting period and engagement of more manpower.
- Sub-standard cocoon harvest and thus less income to farmers.
- Over spacing on the other hand will lead to wastage of feed and fast withering.
- The silkworm larvae do not eat the withered leaf and thus will be unutilised. The larvae will be weak leading to poor cocoon crop.

Frequency of Feeding

As most of the feed (75%) is consumed during 4th and 5th instars, they should be fed atleast four times in 24 hrs and bed should not be left bare at any time. If temperature and humidity can be maintained as recommended, 4 feedings per day in case of leaf feeding and 3 feedings in case of shoot feedings are advocated. However, during raining season the number of feedings depending on the weather conditions can be manipulated or regulated but minimum 2 feedings per day must be provided in raining season. Moreover, there should not be any compromise on the quantum of feed required for a particular stage, failing which the quality of cocoon will be affected considerably. Sufficient quantity of feed should be given, so that few leaves are found in the bed at the time of next feeding. If worms are found exposed with no leaf in the bed that is the sign of underfeeding at the previous feeding. If underfeeding continues, the larvae will be small and weak and eventually will make inferior quality of cocoon besides melted cocoons.

Frequency of Bed Cleaning

Bed cleaning is carried out twice in 3rd instar, daily in 4th and 5th instar in leaf feeding method. Bed cleaning is carried out with the help of bed cleaning nets. In shoot feeding method, bed cleaning is done by hand to remove leaf-over leaves, faecal matter etc., from the rearing bed. First bed cleaning in each instar is carried out after 2 or 3 feeds. This is done by rolling the top shoots with the larvae carefully and transferring them to a clean bed. Then the refuse is removed from the bed and put in a refuse basket or litter container and carried out to the refuse pit. After bed cleaning, hand should be washed with disinfectant and feeding is given immediately. The second bed cleaning is done when larvae are in its half way of development and last cleaning when the larvae starts symptoms of settling for moult. However, the number of bed cleaning is to be carried out in any instar is not very rigid. It may be one or two cleaning more or less depending on the conditions of the rearing bed and prevailing micro-environmental conditions in the rearing rooms. If more feeding is given, bed will be thick and farmer may be forced to clean more times than if correct feeding is given. Thick beds are breeding grounds for germs and therefore if bed is thick, it is to be cleaned immediately. Bed cleaning is mostly carried out with cotton or nylon nets. The net is spread over the rearing bed and one or two feedings are given before the nets are lifted and transferred to a fresh cleaned tray. The silkworm larvae crawl through the meshes in the net and come up to feed the leaves on the nets. The mesh size of the net used for different instars should be 10 mm^2 for 3rd instar and 20 mm^2 for 4th and 5th instar larvae.

Care During Moult

The moulting duration in longer in 4th moult compared to 1st - 3rd moults. Under optimum conditions of temperature (24^{0}C) and humidity (60-70%), the moulting duration of 4th moult is approximately 30 hrs. It is recommended to adopt the following during moult –

- When few worms have stopped eating and raised their head, the quantum of feed should be reduced because the rate of consumption of leaf gradually decreases as larvae starts entering into moult.
- When most of the larvae (90%) stopped eating and their anterior parts of the head are raised and they are motionless, just small quantity of feed cut into small pieces is given to cover the larvae. This is known as spot feeding. If still some larvae are observed eating, they are removed and put in separate tray and feed them until settled for moult.
- After all the larvae have settled for moult, slaked lime powder is dusted evenly on the rearing bed. This helps to dry the left over leaf if any and avoid dampness so that moulting can takes place in dry environment. Lime powder also acts as disinfectant as freshly moulted larval skin needs protection.
- When all the larvae are out of moult, dust lime or bed disinfectant evenly on the bed. Wait for half an hour before giving the first feed to moulted larvae. As the mouth parts of freshly moulted larvae will be delicate, it is advisable to give some what succulent leaf cut into small pieces.
- Give full feed when their appetite increases.

- Any mishandling and bad maintenance of environmental conditions during moulting period may lead to irregular moulting which will affect the larval health and ultimately quality of cocoon.

Larval Protection During Rearing

In silkworm rearing, out break of diseases are closely related to the unhygienic conditions of the rearing bed, rearing room and surroundings. If rearing room and appliances are disinfected before rearing, pathogens are greatly reduced or even eliminated. However, in course of rearing, pathogens can be reintroduced in the rearing room through many means. Larvae pass out the pathogens along with litters, which can contaminate the mulberry leaf in the bed. If healthy larvae consume these contaminated leaves, there is possibility that the larvae will suffer from the disease. To avoid this, the rearing bed, rearing room and surroundings are to be dusted with recommended disinfectant.

(a) *Slaked Lime*: It is very widely used bed disinfectant and drying agent in sericulture. When it is dusted on the silkworm or left over leaves, it absorbs moisture and toxic gases in the rearing bed. When it absorbs moisture and become calcium hydroxide of pH more than 11, and when pathogen comes in contact with it, they will be inactivated and further secondary contamination will be reduced. When lime is applied during moulting period, it dries the bed by absorbing moisture and toxic gases and releasing heat by its exothermic reaction with water molecules. The delicate skin of silkworm during the moulting period will be protected against pathogens by the lime. Further, lime also dries the left over leaves in the bed so that the leaves are not available for the early moulted silkworms, ensuring the uniformity of larvae. Even the residual lime entering into the body of the silkworm through the leaf is not harmful to the silkworm. Hence the application of lime on the silkworm bed improves the micro-climate of the tray in additions to the inactivation of pathogens, which is a very important component in disease management. Lime should be applied 4-5 hrs after last feeding during each moult. This is good for fast and uniform moulting and reduces contamination during moulting. The lime can also be dusted on the freshly moulted larvae to disinfectant their body surface probably contaminated with contaminated leaf and faecal matter. This can be done prior to half an hour of giving first feeding to the moulted larvae. The quantity of lime required for 100 DFLs is about 4-5 kg. This is for drying the bed during moult. Another 3-4 kg is required for disinfecting the freshly moulted larvae if other bed disinfectants are not available. There is no hard and fast rule regarding the quantity of lime to be used during rearing period for various purposes. However, a uniform film of dust of lime needs to be spread. Excess usage of lime is not harmful to silkworms.

(b) *Bed Disinfectant*: The bed disinfectant developed and recommended for use in sericulture during silkworm rearing is Resham Keet Oushad (RKO), Vijetha, Ankush, Suraksha, Sanjeevani, Resham Jyothi, Labex, Rakshak etc. Most of these bed disinfectants are being prepared using lime as base material. Dusting of bed disinfectant helps in reducing the extent of contamination and spread of diseases during silkworm rearing. The method of application of bed disinfectant is as follows –

- Take the bed disinfectant powder on a thin muslin cloth/duster and dust it uniformly over the silkworm larvae in recommended quantity after bed cleaning.
- Bed disinfectants are to be dusted when larvae are out of moult but before feeding.
- It is to be dusted once in every instar after moult except in 5th instar where it is dusted twice, once after 4th moult when it enters in 5th instar and second time on 4th day of 5th instar.
- Do not dust when the larvae are in moult or when the silkworms are in eating stage.

- Feed silkworms after 30 minutes of dusting.
- The dusting should be uniform covering all the silkworms and rearing bed.

The schedule and recommended quantity of disinfectants to be dusted on silkworm is presented in Table 6.5.

Table 6.5: Standard Quantity of Bed Disinfectant Recommended for 100 DFLs

Stage of Larvae	Vijetha/ Ankush (gm)	RKO (gm)	Resham Jyothi (gm)
Out of 1st moult (before resumption)	50	60	35
Out of 2nd moult (before resumption)	150	120	105
Out of 3rd moult (before resumption)	600	580	300
Out of 4th moult (before resumption)	1250	960	840
IV day of 5th instar (after resumption)	2000	1540	2160
Total quantity (gm)	4050	3260	3440

However, these bed disinfectants should be stored in air tight conditions, keep away from the reach of children, use exclusive cloth or the duster for the purpose of dusting and use mask to protect nose, eyes and ears during dusting.

Sex Separation

Some times F1 hybrids raised by sericulture farmers are also utilised for preparation of double hybrids which are now becoming popular in the field. Therefore, for preparation of hybrids, the sexes are to be separated. The distinguishing characters of male and female at different stages is presented in Table 6.6. In India incidentally, none of the authorized parental silkworm breeds are having sex limited markings on their larval body, thus making the job of sex separation apparently impossible during larval stage.

Sex Discrimination of Larvae

The most popular method available for sex separation is based on imaginal buds for sexual organs in pupa and larva besides on sex limited markings. Tazima (1978) reported the best time for discriminating between two sexes in the early fifth instar just after two feedings of fourth moult based on Ishiwata and Harold's imaginary glands. On the ventral side of 8th and 9th abdominal segments sexual markings appear as a pair of milky white spots, one each on the right and left side in 8th and 9th abdominal segments in female. These spots are known as Ishiwata's glands. The anterior pair situated in the 8th abdominal segment is known as Ishiwata's fore gland and the posterior pair in 9th segment is referred as Ishiwata's hind glands. In the male silkworm a small milky white protuberance at the centre of the ventral side between 8th and 9th abdominal segment is observed known as Herold's gland. The male and female can be distinguished based on these glands during early 5th instar larvae (2nd day). Separation of thousands of larvae in this short stipulated period of time is quite difficult on large commercial scale. However, sex discrimination by sexual gland requires skilled technique and has to be conducted by expert workers. Moreover, this method is not very efficient and leads to error, thus has not become a popular practice.

Sex Discrimination of Pupae

Though, the separation of male and female pupae by identification of pupal marking is quite easy, other factors such as cutting of cocoons, enormous engagement of labourers to cut large quantity of cocoons in commercial grainages, the damage caused to pupae while cutting the cocoons, damage by dermestid beetle on the naked pupae and due to handling makes this method too labourious and cumbersome besides this practice requires cutting of all the available cocoons leading to considerable loss in quantity of silk of both the parents. Again the mistake committed in the identification of the sexes cannot be ruled out. So, after emergence undesirable sexes not required for hybrid preparation must be picked. The result due to all these problems is that practically no sex separation is usually carried before emergence in the grainages. In this processes again considerable quantum of laying produced are selfed seed rather than hybrid and also pierced cocoons fetch very less or negligible return.

Sex separation at pupal stage on the basis of weight differences by means of brine/salt assortment is also available but here again cutting open of all cocoons, pupa and shell separation, soaking the pupa in salt solution and removing it from the container etc., requires additional labour besides wasting of huge quantity of either sexes not required for hybrid/seed preparation and hence this practice has not attracted the attention of breeders and grainures. Kataoka *et al.* (1973) stated that the sex separation at pupal stage is possible by measuring the change in the electric capacity but it varies with the pupal growth besides the value of the electric capacity. It somewhat also varied according to distance between two plates of the test capacitor and size of the cocoons tested, rather large values were reported in small size cocoons measured in narrow distance.

Table 6.6: Distinguishing Characters between Male and Female Silkworm

Male	Female
Larva Presence of a tiny milky white follicular structure called Harold's gland in the centre line of the ventral side of the junction of 8th and 9th abdominal segments. As the larvae grow, the spot merges with the skin color	Presence of small round spots on the ventral side of both the left and right margins of the 8th and 9th the 8th and 9th abdominal segments called Ishiwata's gland. These spots slowly fade out with growth and finally disappear
Cocoon Volume: Smaller; Weight: Lighter Shell ratio: Higher	Volume: Larger; Weight: Heavier Shell ratio: Lower
Pupa Cuticle is slightly darker in color Smaller in size Abdomen narrow and small Posterior end tapering Presence of dot like marking in the centre of ninth abdominal segment on the ventral side Lighter in weight	Cuticle is lighter in color Comparatively bigger in size Abdomen broad and large Posterior end blunt Presence of a longitudinal slit 'X' marking on the ventral side of 8th abdominal segment extending from anterior to posterior margin of the segment Heavier in weight

Sex Discrimination of Cocoons

Ming (1994) observed that when moths emerged from their uncut cocoons, the average rate of egg production can be approximately 20 per cent higher than when cocoons are cut opened because the risk of injury due to handling of pupae is reduced. Since female cocoon are generally heavier than the males of the same race, use can be made of these differences to separate the female cocoons from the male by cocoon weight differences.

The separation of sexes based on cocoon weight differences in male and female has following advantages –

- The unwanted component (male in case of multivoltine and females in case of bivoltine) of seed can be disposed off for raw silk production.
- Selfing can be prevented which otherwise may lead to deterioration in the quality of hybrid seed.
- Number of trays to be attended reduced by 35-45 per cent and thus increases the efficiency of skilled workers.
- The potency of bivoltine male moth is protected otherwise would mate with females and ejaculate once by the time they are picked up.
- Emission of moth scales (dust) a health hazard in commercial grainages is reduced significantly as the male component of one of the parent is eliminated.
- There is no need of cocoon cutting.
- As the pupae are inside the intact cocoons, the risk of preservation of pupae in the naked form is eliminated and thus mortality during preservation is reduced considerably.
- 35-45 per cent unwanted components (male or female) is disposed off leading to reduction in the accumulation of pierced cocoons.
- There is immediate realisation of sale proceeds from the cocoons sold for reeling.

Before employing sexing based on cocoon weight differences, few samples of cocoons are taken at random from the same batch of the seed cocoons. The weight of criterion cocoon is determined based on the ranges of the weight between male and female cocoons. This is used as differentiation weight for sex separation of seed cocoons. Cocoons that are heavier than the criterion weight belong to the female group and those lighter to the male. Cocoons of the same weight as the criterion cocoons belong to the mixed group of both sexes.

The correct evaluation of criterion cocoon has considerable effect on the work as a whole. The criterion weight must maintain a rate of sexing of 90 per cent or higher. At the same time, the sexing rate of mixed group should be controlled to 10 per cent or less. If this requirement is not met, the sex separation by cocoon weight differences will be of no significance. Studies conducted indicated that there is inherent error exiting in the population, which vary in accordance to the crop status and season. The inherent error is primarily due to overlapping of cocoon weight of male and females. The error could be reduced to a considerable limit, if separate cut-off points are determined for males and females besides introducing an intermediate range, wherein the cocoons are required to be physically verified.

For determining the cut-off points, cocoons are taken at random from the sample, cut opened, sexed, recorded weight individually with the help of electronic digital monopan balance, values are arranged in ascending or descending order, and cut-off points are decided. There are usually three systems to determine the cut-off points –

(a) *Percentile Frequency and Subjective Analysis*: By percentile frequency and subjective analysis, the frequency table could be constructed. Based on higher percentile value cut-off points for male are determined in contrast to female cut-off points which are determined based on initial percentile value. In this way two cut-off points, one for males and other for females with three distinct groups' *viz;* above percentile value - male, below percentile value - female and intermediate percentile value - mixed group (male and female) are formed. This intermediate group can be sex separated manually. This one is the most efficient method of sex determination based on cocoon weight differences.

(b) *Mean of Male and Female*: By calculating mean of both the sexes in the population to determine the cut-off points. In this method, only one cut-off point is determined and the values above the mean are considered as female while below as male. This is not very efficient method because chances of error are more due to single cut-off point and inherent error.

(c) *Standard Deviation*: By addition or subtraction of ¼ populations in Standard Deviation (S.D.) the cut-off points are decided in the percentile procedure. If only males are required for hybrid preparation ¼ population SD is subtracted from the population mean, in contrast to the addition of per cent ¼ population SD if only females are required for the purpose. By adopting this method, error can be reduced considerably and can be brought below 7 per cent.

By using the single digital balance, the efficiency is much higher as it does not take much time to display the weight. Whereas in sensitive balance with 10 mg accuracy *i.e.*, two digit balance, it takes time to display the correct weight and thus affects, the speed of weighment of cocoons. A skilled worker can sex separate about 10,000-12,000 bivoltine and 6,000-8,000 multivoltine cocoons in an eight hours shift.

By adopting the procedure 50 per cent cocoons of multivoltine (male cocoons) and 50 per cent cocoons of Bivoltine (female cocoons) can be saved while preparing MV x BV hybrid combination. These intact cocoons could be sent to reeling for commercial silk production fetching higher return to the grainure.

Sex separation at larval and cocoon stages is the best proposition due to the following advantages –

- Cocoon cutting is avoided thereby reducing the labour significantly. Damage to pupa during cocoon cutting is also avoided.
- Pupa inside the shell is protected well otherwise, emergence percentage is affected and moths loose vigour if soiled due to urination.
- When only one of the parents is utilised for hybridization, as in cross breed egg production, the unwanted component could be more appropriately used for reeling.

Disease Prevention During Silkworm Rearing

The mulberry silkworm, *Bombyx mori* L., like any other insect, is prone to various diseases occurring in nature. Having been domesticated over centuries, it developed total dependence on man who has to take care of it. During its growth, the silkworm comes in contact with various pathogens, and under the influence of the environment, the pathogen's capability to infect and its own capability to resist or succumb or co-exist, infection occurs. When the physiological equilibrium of the host is lost with the interference of the pathogen, a disease is said to occur. The threat of the disease is associated with the factors like poor quality of mulberry leaf, unfavorable weather conditions, lack of independent rearing houses for effective disinfections, poor hygiene and above all faulty rearing practices. In small and short-lived insects, it is difficult to treat and cure the disease besides which shall also be uneconomical. Prevention is therefore suggested in containing silkworm diseases. Of the various diseases, viral diseases (Nuclear polyhedrosis, Cytoplasmic polyhedrosis, Infectious flacherie and Densonucleosis), bacterial diseases (Bacterial septicaemia, Bacterial toxicosis and Bacterial diseases of digestive tract.); fungal diseases (White Muscardine, Green Muscardine, Black Muscardine, Brown Muscardine and Aspergillosis) and protozoan disease (Pebrine) are causing considerable damage to silkworm crop.

All diseases of silkworm *viz*; protozoan, viral, bacterial and fungal are common in all rearing seasons. The improved rearing technology, package of practices for mulberry cultivation and preventive measures followed for diseases have improved the cocoon crop position. However, crop losses due to diseases in tropics continue to above 15-20 per cent. The causes of all these diseases and their causative agents, route of infection, source of contamination, pathogen resistance, symptoms of disease, alternate host, preventive measures etc., are discussed in detail by Khan *et al.* (2011). These silkworm diseases are difficult to be identified by external features during early instars as well as till late fifth instars or until they develop clear external symptoms. Therefore, their preventive measures and method of microscopical test for identification of the disease is presented hereunder in brief –

Preventive Measures

- Silkworm rearing rooms, mulberry leaf storage rooms, mounting rooms and rearing and mounting equipments should be thoroughly disinfected.
- Surface disinfection of silkworm eggs before brushing is to be carried out.
- Maintenance of proper temperature and humidity according to the requirement as per age and stage of development of larvae.
- Maintenance of proper hygienic conditions.
- Feeding nutritious mulberry leaves especially as per age and stage of developing silkworms.
- Provide constant fresh air circulation.
- Careful removal of diseased larvae and their proper disposal suitably by burning or by burying. The litter pit should be away from the rearing house.
- Change of infected seat paper and tray.
- Provide sufficient spacing according to the age and stage of larvae.
- Careful handling especially after moult.
- Keep bed thin and dry especially during rainy season.

- Application of bed disinfectant to prevent secondary contamination and spread of diseases *viz;* Resham Keet Oushad (RKO), Vijetha, Labex, Resham Jyothi etc.
- Proper incubation of silkworm eggs.
- Avoid growing mulberry in phosphorus deficient soil, under shade and high alkaline and acidic soil condition.
- Soiled and diseased leaves moist with raindrops should also be avoided for feeding.
- Spray of 0.3 per cent slaked lime solution in addition to usual disinfection procedure is recommended in case of high incidence of disease in the previous crop.
- Avoid cold storage of freshly hatched larvae.
- Avoid overcrowding.
- Avoid accumulation of faeces in rearing beds.
- Larvae must be prevented for swelling of toxic substances.
- Use anti-muscardine agents/bed disinfectant like Labex, Formalin chaff and Dithane M45 or Captan with lavigated china clay (Kaolin) for prevention of fungal disease.
- Bavistin, Bayleton, Vitavax, Dithane M-45, Daconil and formalin are found controlling the aspergillosis of silkworm.

Microscopical Identification of Polyhedral Causing Viral Diseases

- Make a smear of polyhedra on a slide and air dry.
- Fix in methyl alcohol for 5 sec and air dry.
- Stain in Giemsa for 45-60 minutes (1 or 2 drops of stock giemsa stain to 1 ml of distilled water).
- Wash in distilled water.
- Air dry or blot dry and mount in DPX.
- Examine under high power of microscope.
- Polyhedra stained in violet blue.

Microscopical Identification of Bacterial Diseases (Crystal – violet saffranin method)

- Make a bacterial smear on a slide and heat it by passing the slide on the flame.
- Immerse the slide in ammonium oxalate crystal violet stain for one minute.
- Rinse the slide in running tap water for 5 seconds.
- Rinse quickly with 'Gram Iodine' solution and immerse in it for one minute.
- Dip the slide in 'n-propyl alcohol' for one minute and give three changes separately for one minute in each.
- Counter stain in saffranin for one minute.
- Mount in DPX and observe under oil immersion.
- Gram-positive bacteria take blue stain and gram-negative red stain.

Pebrine Disease

Isolation, purification and identification of spores from the host are the first step in the study of pebrine disease and its management. Following centrifugal procedure (Fujiwara's method) of microscopical examination is carried out for spore isolation and identification in order to monitor the disease –

- Take 20 larvae in a cup of domestic mixer.
- Add 80 ml of 0.6 per cent potassium carbonate solution (K_2CO_3).
- Homogenize the larvae for 1-2 minutes at 10,000 r.p.m. This ensures liberation of spores from the tissues into the medium facilitating more accurate detection of spores during microscopical examination.
- After homogenizing, the contents (homogenate) are transferred into a glass beaker and are allowed to settle for 2-5 minutes. This facilitates to separate host tissues from the liquid portion of homogenate for easy filtration.
- Filter the homogenate by using absorbent cotton or muslin cloth. Volume of filtrate recovered will be around 70 ml.

- Transfer the filtrate into 100 ml capacity of centrifuge tube through funnel. All the centrifuge tubes should be evenly balanced, capped and loaded into the centrifuge machine.
- Centrifugate the filtrate at 3000 r.p.m. for 3-5 minutes to facilitate sedimentation of spores.
- Remove the centrifuge tube from the centrifuge machine.
- Discard slowly the supernatant solution.
- Dissolve the sediment by shaking with a few drops (2-3 drops) of K_2CO_3 or by using a cyclomixer (10-15 seconds) or with a glass rod, which facilitates uniform dissolving.
- Take this smear from the centrifuge tube on the micro-slide, put the cover slip and examine under 600x magnification of microscope.
- Minimum 5 microscopic fields should be examined per smear to detect the presence of pebrine spores.
- Two testers to ensure the detection of pebrine spores may perform microscopical examination.
- If pebrine spores are detected, the entire batch is to be destroyed by burning.

Preparation of Permanent Slide of Pebrine Spores

- Make a thin smear on a glass slide and air dry.
- Fix in methyl alcohol for 2-3 minutes.
- Air-dry or blots dry the smear.
- Dilute giemsa stock solution (1 drop giemsa + 1 ml of distilled water), and stain the smear for 45-60 minutes.
- Wash in distilled water.
- Air dry or blot dry.
- Mount in DPX and examine with 600 magnification of microscope.
- In giemsa stain, pebrine spore appears as pinkish violet or bluish oval body.

Detection of Pebrine Spores in Soil/Dust

- Collect dust from the rearing house and equipments.
- Take 5 gm of the soil sample in a beaker and add 20 ml (1:4) of 0.6 per cent Potassium carbonate solution. Stir it thoroughly for 2 minutes. Allow the suspension to settle for 15-20 minutes.
- Centrifuge the supernatant for 5 minutes at 10,000 r.p.m.
- Collect the sediment.
- Take a drop of distilled water on a glass slide and a small quantity of sediment with a glass rod or brush.
- Add a tiny drop of Indian ink, mount and examine.

Detection of Pebrine Spores on Mulberry Leaves

- Wash 10-15 mulberry leaves in 100 ml of water.
- Centrifuge the wash for 8-10 minutes at 10,000 r.p.m.
- Discard the supernatant.
- Take a drop of distilled water on a glass slide and small quantity of the sediment with a glass rod or brush.
- Add a tiny drop of Indian ink, mount and examine.

Detection of Pebrine Spores in Egg-shell/Eggs/Un-hatched Eggs

- Collect head/body pigmented stage eggs/hatched eggshells/un-hatched eggs into a porcelain/glass mortar and add 0.6 per cent Potassium carbonate solution and grind thoroughly.
- After settling, filtering and centrifuging, examine the sediments after dissolving the same.

Detection of Pebrine Spores in Litters

- Collect 5 gm of litter in a mortar and add 40 ml 0.6 per cent potassium carbonate solution (8 times the weight of litter) and homogenize by grinding. If the resultant homogenate turns out to be viscous, add a few drops of HCI to reduce viscosity.
- After settling, filtering and centrifuging dissolve the sediment and observe under microscope.

Maintenance of Hygiene

- Avoid borrowing of rearing appliances.
- Do not use rearing equipments without disinfections.
- Avoid overlapping rearing.
- Maintain personnel and rearing hygiene.
- Restrict the entry of persons into the rearing house.
- Silkworm eggs should be disinfected with 2 per cent formalin before head pigmentation stage.
- Any person entering the rearing house must disinfect foot and hand before entering.
- A foot mat soaked in 2 per cent bleaching powder should be placed at the entrance and person entering the rearing house should step on to this.
- Wash hands in 2 per cent bleaching powder in 0.3 per cent slaked lime solution.
- Replace the disinfectant every day.
- Diseased/unequal or diseased suspected larvae must be picked from the rearing tray and disposed into 5 per cent bleaching powder in slaked lime in basin. Basin must be covered with lid.
- Diseased larvae should be picked by forks or sticks. If it is picked by hand, disinfectant the hand by washing in 2 per cent bleaching powder in 0.3 per cent slaked lime solution.
- Perform bed cleaning using bed-cleaning net and these nets should be disinfected every day after use by dipping in 2 per cent formalin solution for 10 minutes.
- Bed refuse should be collected on vinyl sheet and transferred into manure pit. Vinyl sheet must be disinfected every day by dipping in 2 per cent bleaching powder in 0.3 per cent slaked lime solution.
- Silkworms should always be reared on rearing sheet paper (newspaper).
- Wipe the floor after bed cleaning with 2 per cent bleaching powder in 0.3 per cent slaked lime solution.

- Dust the bed disinfectant as per schedule, quantity and precautions. Feed the larvae after 30 minutes of bed disinfections.
- Mulberry leaf should not be stored in rearing house, instead store in a separate disinfected room.
- Provide recommended spacing, sufficient ventilation, good quality and quantity of mulberry leaf for healthy and robust growth of larvae.
- Spray bleaching powder in mounting place.
- Avoid injury to silkworms while rearing and mounting.
- Pick diseased and non-spinning larvae from the mountages and dispose them into 2 per cent bleaching powder in 0.3 per cent slaked lime solution in a basin.

CHAPTER 7

Mounting and Mountages

Of the many contributing factors responsible for the production of quality cocoons, rearing and mounting environment, type of mountages used, rearing season and racial characteristic of the breed/hybrid plays a major role. Picking and transferring of mature (ripe) silkworms larvae to the cocooning frames to spin cocoon is known as mounting. Even if silkworm crop is healthy, unscientific mounting methods like transferring of immature silkworm larvae to cocooning frames, use of poor quality of mountages, not regulating and maintaining micro-climatic conditions during spinning of larvae may result in inferior quality of cocoon and poor harvest. Mounting is the last activity of rearing. Lack of knowledge in identification of mature larvae, mounting time, mounting methods and mountages may lead to production of poor quality of cocoons.

Physiological Characteristics of Mature Silkworm

The characteristics of mature or ripe silkworm appear by the end of the last instars of normally developed silkworm. When silkworm ripens, it stops feeding and looks for a suitable place to spin cocoons. The characteristic of approximately mature silkworms is –

- The water content in the larval body decreases from 85 per cent to about 75 per cent and excessive water is excreted together with its faeces.
- Silkworm loses its appetite and finally stops eating.
- The faeces become softer and can be crushed with finger-tips.
- The larvae appear translucent first in the thoracic region, which later develops towards the abdomen.
- The anterior part of the body becomes thinner than rest of the body.
- It raises its head restlessly.
- It bends its anterior portion of the body in semi-circle and moves its head freely in an arc form.
- Generally, a mature silkworm shows negative geotropism or apogeotropism *i.e.,* crawls upward along the wall or rearing bed/stand.
- Mature larvae crawl here and there to find suitable site for cocooning.
- In mass rearing, if about 40 per cent of larvae shows maturation, all the larvae can be collected at the same time for mounting.

Mature silkworm larvae (50 DFLs or 20,000 larvae) discharge approximately 46 liters urine during entire spinning period (Table 7.1). This increases the moisture/humidity at the spinning sites which needs to be removed from the mounting place as soon as possible by providing good ventilation with the help of providing sufficient ventilators and windows at the spinning site.

Silk gland is the source of silk. Silk gland is transformed labial gland and ectodermic in origin having three distinct and functional parts – the posterior, the middle and the anterior with 500, 250 and 300 gland cells respectively at each side with approximately 2000 gland cells altogether. It increases 1.6×10^5 fold from hatching to full grown larvae without any cell division. During the growth of silkworm

Table 7.1: Water Released by Mature Silkworm Larvae During Spinning (50 DFLs or 20,000 Larvae)

Contents		Water Discharge (liter)	Water Discharge (%)
Water	Urine	7.8	16.96
	Water in faeces	4.5	09.78
	Total	12.3	26.74
Water vapour	Solidification of liquid silk	230	50.00
	Respiration	10.7	23.26
	Total	33.7	73.26
	Grand Total	46.0	100.00

larvae, it increases 20, 6, 5, 6 and 40 folds in 1st, 2nd, 3rd, 4th and 5th instars respectively and finally accounts for 40 per cent of the larval body weight. Posterior part secretes silk substance known as 'fibroin', while the middle part serves as reservoir for receiving the fibroin from the posterior silk gland. It also secretes around the fibroin, a natural gummy substance known as 'sericin'. These substances when coming into contact with air harden into silk filament. Posterior end of the gland is closed while fore end joins together to a common excretory duct opening into the spinneret. The major components contain in the cocoon shell are presented in Table 7.2.

Table 7.2: Chemical Composition of Silk Filament

S. No.	Materials	Percentage
1.	Fibroin	70.0-80.0
2.	Sericin	18.0-28.0
3.	Carbohydrates	1.2-1.6
4.	Fat and Wax	0.5-1.0%
5.	Colouring matter, minerals and Ash	1.0-1.4

The pH of fibroin is 2.1-2.5, having a chemical formula of C15 H26 N5 O6, while sericin has a pH of 3.8-4.2 with a chemical formula of C15 H25 N5 O6. There are 18 amino acids in fibroin and sericin *i.e.*, Glycine, Alanine, Valine, Leucine,

Isoleucine, Phenlalanine, Methionine, Cystine, Tyrosine, Tryptophane, Proline, Aspartic acid, Glutamic acid, Threonine, Serine, Histidine, Lysine and Arginine. These 18 amino acids can be categorised into three type's *viz*; neutral, acidic and alkaline amino acids. Neutral amino acids are Glycine, Alanine, Leucine, Isoleucine, Proline, Phenlalanine, Cystine, Valine, Serine, Threonine and Tyrosine. Alkaline amino acid groups are Arginine, Histidine and Lysine. And amino acid groups are Methionine, Aspartic acid and Glutamic acid.

Cocoon Formation

Silkworm cocooning process may be divided into three stages as shown below –

- Mature silkworm that appears translucent raises its head and crawls here and there to find a suitable cocooning site. It first spins some silk waves into the mounting to form a framework of a cocoon and then continues to spin to form a cocoon net. Irregular and loose silk is spun to thicken the cocoon net and gradually cocoon frame is formed.
- The larval body bends towards its back, its abdominal legs are fixed on the internal wall of the cocoon cavity, its head swings left and right to spin silk.
- The larvae swings head like 'S' or '8' inside the cocoon shell and crawl around to make cocoon shell thicker gradually from inside.
- The pattern of spun silk filament is continuous in the shape of number '8' or letter 'S'.
- The larva stretches the caudal end and discharges the urine which is about 0.5 ml/larva in the forms of drops with semisolid faeces.
- Secretion of large quantity of silk makes the silkworm shrink remarkably. The swinging of its head slows down and finally loses the rhythm of swinging. As a result, a thin layer of pupal covering is formed. Finally, towards the upper end of the cocoon, larva secretes the last silk material forming a loose and soft cocoon top.

- The time required for spinning silk to make a cocoon from beginning to the end is usually 48 hrs at 25⁰C, but it varies with the breed/hybrid and temperature at the time of spinning.
- If environment is too humid, drying of silk filament excreted from spinneret is slow resulting in poor reelability.
- Thus, the cocooning process is completed and the larva becomes ready for pupation.
- Therefore, mounting should not be delayed, when the larvae get matured; mounting should be done in a place where it can be handled easily. Mounting place should be kept dry with good aeration.
- If mounting is delayed for more than 12-18 hrs, defective and flimsy cocoons are formed.

Environmental Conditions

The spinning silkworms are very sensitive to physical disturbances like temperature, humidity, air current and photoperiod (Huang, 1983). During mounting, optimum temperature and humidity must be 24-25⁰C and 60-70 per cent respectively. Care must be taken to avert the temperature, rising above 28⁰C or humidity increasing to more than 90 per cent, because such temperature and humidity are detrimental to quality of cocoon. Since temperature and humidity exert the greatest influence on the cocoon quality during the initial 50 hrs after mounting, attention must be paid to control the microclimatic conditions during the first 50 hrs of spinning (Manishankar *et al.* 2008).

The worms should be mounted at the time of proper maturity to harvest uniform cocoons. If environmental conditions during spinning are not optimum, it will lead to a neatness defects of raw silk also. Neatness declines remarkably if mounting is performed at high temperature exceeding 28⁰C at a humidity of more than 90 per cent. Reelability is the most important property of cocoons for raw silk production and is vulnerable to change due to mounting conditions. If temperature and humidity in the mounting rooms are 28⁰C and 94 per cent respectively, reelability sometimes drops as low as 20 per cent lower than the value attainable with the mounting room temperature held at 25^{0}C and Relative Humidity of 70 per cent. Therefore, adequate care must be taken about the temperature and humidity during mounting. Too high temperature makes larvae hurriedly build cocoons, so that double cocoon increases and the cocoons thus produced have loose cocoon shell and inferior quality. Too low temperature slows down the speed of cocooning and pupation. The cocoons are often short, thin or perforated at both ends and lose its normal colour, texture and luster. Non-cocooning silkworms will also increase. Low humidity causes double layered cocoons and loose cocoons. Therefore temperature and relative humidity during spinning/mounting of silkworm larvae in the mounting room should be maintained at the optimum level (Ramachandra *et al.* 2001).

Air current has an indirect effect on the quality of cocoons. Its function is to dispel the high moisture in the mounting room and introduce the dry air from outside. It can also lower the temperature in the mounting room. In the beginning of mounting, strong wind is to be avoided to make the larvae to find suitable cocooning site as quickly as possible. After 24 hrs of mounting, when most of the larvae have built thin cocoon shell, an air current with 0.5-1.0 m/sec should be provided to dispel the high moisture to improve cocoon quality. Strong air current above 1.0 m/sec causing crowding of mature silkworms resulting in more number of double cocoons. During rainy season more than recommended air current is must to dispel the excess accumulated humidity from the mounting hall and vice-versa during summer and winter. Mounting rooms requires moderate and even illumination and strong light causes crowding of silkworm at one side and finally results in formation of double cocoons or uneven thickness cocoons. Complete darkness will slow down the spinning process resulting in low quality cocoons. The combined effect of temperature, humidity and air current during cocooning on reelability is presented in Table 7.3 (Rajan and Himantharaj, 2005). The results presented show that low humidity (60%) and air current of 50 cm/sec are adequate for obtaining a good reelability of above 90 per cent.

Ripe worms are very sensitive to light. They evade the strong light over 100 lux, but prefer dim light of about 15-30 lux. Temperature, humidity and air current affect reelability of cocoons in mutually interactive manner and therefore, they should be maintained to the optimum level for better reelability and quality of cocoon.

Table 7.3: Combined Effect of Temperature, Humidity and Air Current during Spinning time on Cocoon Reelability

Temperature (°C)	Relative Humidity (%)	Air Current (cm/sec)	Reelability (%)
20	65	0	75
		50	90
	90	0	78
		50	92
25	65	0	92
		50	96
	90	0	55
		50	90
30	65	0	85
		50	93
	90	0	30
		50	80

Mountages

Mountages plays very important role in the production of quality cocoons. Type of mountages besides mounting material used for spinning of cocoons determines the uniformity and production of quality cocoons. An analysis of crop data of silkworm clearly indicates that among the many factors that contribute for a good yield, mounting material used for spinning of cocoons play an important role. Even if silkworm crop is healthy, wrong mounting methods, spinning conditions, mounting density and bad types of mountages can result in formation of inferior quality of cocoons. Moreover, the aim of mounting material is to provide much cocooning space to ripe silkworm larvae with engagement of reduced manpower. Following points, therefore, must be taken into consideration while selecting a cocooning frame –

- Cocooning space should be sufficient between frame works.
- Easy handling and light in weight.
- Ridges and furrows should be firm and uniformly distributed.
- Surface should be rough to get grip for larvae while spinning.
- Mountages should be cheap, sturdy and durable.
- Manpower required for mounting and harvesting of cocoons should be at reduced level so as to save labour and raise working efficiency.
- Better aeration between ridges and furrows for reduction of humidity during spinning to improve the reelability.
- Should be easy for thorough disinfection and convenient for storage when not in use.
- Mountages should be convenient to conduct the operation of mounting and harvesting.
- Should be non-corrosive and non-biodegradable.
- Better if suitable for self-mounting.
- Should have certain hygroscopicity to absorb moisture caused by excretion of urine.

Different types of mountages used in different countries and in India (Chandrakanth *et al.* 2004) are presented in Table 7.4.

Different types of mountages used and popular in India (Mathur and Qadri, 2010) are presented below with their description.

- Mulberry twigs/Straw/grass/mustard hay mountages.
- Plastic collapsible mountages.
- Pine-shoot let mountages.
- Plastic bottle brush mountages.

Table 7.4: Different Types of Mountages used in Different Countries

Types of Mountages	Mechanism	Country	Space for Mounting
Rotary card board mountage	Rotation and hanging made up of card board	Japan	Individual cell
Folded straw mountage	Fixed and waved shaped	Japan	Common
Centipede mountage (Cylindrical or domed shaped)	Fixed, Hanging vertically or horizontally, Made out of bamboo, coconut, plastic with rope and iron	China, Thailand, Vietnam, Nepal, India	Common
Twigs (Mulberry, red gram, cotton) mountages	Fixed, standing vertically, made out of brush wood	France, India	Common
Plastic collapsible mountages (Wave shaped)	Fixed, standing vertically or horizontal in use	India, China, Japan	Common
Eucalyptus, mango leaves	Fixed, standing vertically or horizontal in use	India	Common
Chandrike	Fixed, standing in use, made of bamboo	India	Common

- Square-frame mountages.
- Centipede like mountages.
- Rotary mountages.
- Traditional bamboo spiral mountages.

Of these, plastic mountages, bamboo spiral mountages and rotary mountages are mostly in use in different sericultural tracts of the country. The type of mountages used may affect the cocoon quality. The structure of mountages directly affects the spinning and cocooning of silkworm. The microclimate in the mountages also affects the cocoon quality in general and its reelability in particular.

Rotary Card Board Mountage

Rotary card board mountages are used mostly in Japan (Kotoku, 1993). It comprises of 10 card board frames of 55 cm × 40 cm size with 13 rows and 12 sections having 156 cells of 4.5 × 3 × 3 cm size. A set of card board frames are accommodated in a wooden frame. Size of wooden frame is 58 cm x 48 cm and length is about 120 cm to accommodate 10 mountages at an interval of 8 cm. There are two hooks on both the sides of wooden frame to hang the mountages from ceiling for free rotation. Hence, it is called rotary mountages. Each frame has the capacity of 1560 larvae to be mounted but 89 per cent of it *i.e.,* 1200 larvae are usually mounted on the frame. As there is uniform and equal size of cells for each larva to spin cocoons, the cocoons thus formed are also uniform in size and shape. There is no chance of formation of double cocoons or soiling of cocoons due to dead larvae and loss of silk thread in the form of floss.

Old newspaper is spread on the floor and rotary mountage frames are arranged on it horizontally. About 1200 matured silkworm larvae are collected and transferred to the frame. About 4-6 hrs are allowed for the larvae to climb on the mounting frame. When all the larvae climb on the mountage and start spinning, the entire frame is lifted and suspended from the ceiling. Mountages are rotated to 180 degree for uniform distribution of larvae in the mountages. Mountages are prevented from rotation after a day to avoid breaking of filament. Harvest of cocoon is easier and saves manpower also. The cocoons are uniform in size and of good quality and same size and shape. The initial cost of rotary mountages is very high and is out of reach of poor and medium sericulture farmers (Dandin *et al.* 2005). Also it required separate mounting space which farmers mostly do not have. However, this type of mountages is gaining popularity in breeding and silkworm seed production technology at the government establishments.

Plastic Bottle Brush Mountage

Different types of bottle brush mountages are available depending on the material used. They can be made up of plastic, bamboo or coconut broomsticks. Plastic bottle brush mountages are made of plastic and are machine made. The mountage is used for self mounting. When 40 per cent larvae are matured and starts spinning, the bottle brush mountages are lined up on the rearing bed. The mountages are lifted after 4-6 hrs when larvae climb on it and hanged vertically on the roof or between the two ropes or two wires stretched horizontally in the space above the rearing bed or tied between two walls. One meter of mountage can accommodate approximately 450 t0 500 matured larvae to spin the cocoons. Urinated cocoons are minimum and reelability is improved due to good aeration during cocooning period. Plastic bottle brush mountages are durable and can be disinfected easily. However, this type of mountage is not popular among the farmer due to high cost and also not available locally.

Bamboo Spiral Mountage

Indian farmers use mountages made of bamboo called chandrike. It consists of two bamboo support and on it bamboo net is woven as tapes at a distance of 5 cm spirally. Mountages may be of different sizes but they are mostly preferred in the size of 6 feet in length and 4 feet in width which generally can accommodate 900 to 1000 larvae depending the breeds and hybrids mounted. Matured silkworm larvae ready for spinning are transferred @ 40-50 larvae/sq. feet. Chandrike mounted with larvae are kept at an angle of 45^0 to allow urine to fall on the ground and to prevent staining of cocoons caused by urination. Mountages are turned upside down after 8-12 hrs of mounting for equal distribution of larvae in the chandrike. This type of mountages is very popular with Indian farmers. However, the durability of these mountages less and hygienic conditions can not be maintained and these are difficult to disinfect properly to the satisfaction. Separate space is required for mounting and storage of chandrike when not in use which most of the Indian sericulture farmers do not possess. These traditional mountages are usually bigger in size and hence handling is not very easy but as these mountages can be easily made by the farmers and hence is cheaper.

Plastic Collapsible Mountage

Plastic collapsible mountages are made of plastic mesh (8 cm long and 6 cm wide) having 11 folds of 6 cm height with length of 3 feet x 2 feet to accommodate 350-400 matured silkworm larvae during spinning. At the time of mounting, old newspapers are spread below the mountage in the wooden/plastic tray to facilitate urine absorption. In self mounting method, the plastic collapsible mountages are kept directly on the bed with uniformly arranged folds when 30-40 per cent larvae start spinning. Matured larvae crawled up and spin cocoons. In pick up method, the mountage is arranged in the trays and matured larvae @ 40-50 larvae/sq. feet are transferred on the mountages. These mountages are very light in weight, less space is required for storage, due to its collapsible nature, easy for handing and disinfection and above all do not require additional space for mounting. These are durable and help in maintaining the hygienic conditions besides production of uniform cocoons. However, due to repeated use, it loses its shape, size, peak and corrugated nature resulting in uneven space for making cocoon. It can be damaged by rodents very easily.

Mulberry Twigs/Dried Grass/Straw Mountage

When 30-40 per cent of silkworm larvae becomes mature and starts spinning, mango twigs, eucalyptus twigs, mulberry twigs, mustard hey or dried grass are spread over them in three dimensional directions. Matured silkworm larvae crawl through the bed on the mountage to spin cocoon. This method is simple; labour and time saving but size and shape of the cocoon can not be maintained. Chances of double cocoon and defective cocoon are also more. Harvesting of cocoons requires more time and material used for mounting can not be reused and be mulched in soil for getting organic manure.

Evaluation of different types of mountages has been carried out by Central Sericultural Research and Training Institute, Mysore in the laboratory at an optimum temperature of 26-27^{0}C and humidity of 65-70 per cent. Their comparative performance is presented in Table 7.5.

Table 7.5: Comparative Efficiency of Different Types of Mountages (Rajan and Himantharaj, 2005)

Type of Mount-age	Cocooning (%)	Defective Cocoon (%)	Floss (%)	Single Cocoon Weight (g)	Single Shell Weight (g)	Shell Ratio (%)	Average Filament Length (mtr)	Reliability (%)
Rotary	95.22	1.96	1.76	1.92	0.377	20.15	1039	89.96
Plastic bottle brush	93.46	5.92	2.82	2.02	0.389	19.15	962	87.29
Bamboo bottle brush	90.74	6.02	2.80	1.99	0.396	19.53	'934	85.39
Plastic collapsible	89.35	7.96	3.31	2.03	0.406	19.76	884	81.63
Paddy straw	76.03	14.53	3.46	2.03	0.388	19.09	850	83.89
Chan-drike	90.23	9.12	4.10	1.89	0.388	20.38	993	81.36

Mounting Time

Mounting time also has an influence on the production of quality cocoons. Mounting of silkworm larvae too early or too late have adverse effects. Too early mounting often results in light cocoon weight, low cocoon-shell ratio, more spotted cocoons, etc. It also increases the number of wandering silkworms in mountages besides non-cocooning silkworms.

Mounting Methods

(i) *Hand Picking Method:* The most commonly used method in practice is picking of individual matured larvae by hand and mounting on the mounting frames. When more than 40 per cent larvae attain maturity, all larvae are picked and transferred onto the mountages for spinning of cocoons. However, this method is more effective when worms attain uniform growth and maturity. After 6-8 hrs of mounting, if overcrowding of larvae is observed in the mountages, extra larvae are picked from the mountages and mounted in separate mountage. However, this is time and labour consuming method. Since the silkworm larvae are picked by hand one by one and mounted on the mountages, the density of mounted worms can be controlled leading to reduced double cocoon formation. Also diseased larvae can easily be sorted out which ensures formation of uniform and healthy cocoons.

(ii) *Shaking-off Method:* When only few silkworms are found mature, they are mounted by picking. When half of the larvae become mature, mulberry branches or the net for the grown silkworms are spread on the rearing bed. After most of the larvae have crawled onto them, transfer and shake the larvae off the branches or nets in the hand tray. From here, the larvae are then gently spread onto mountages. Shoot rearing method is more suitable for this type of mounting wherein shake the larvae off the shoots directly.

(iii) *Natural Mounting Method:* Since, the mature silkworm larvae have the habit of moving upward, mountages be directly placed on rearing bed. In this method when more than 40 per cent larvae becomes mature and symptoms of spinning appears, cocooning frames *viz;* bottle brush mountage, plastic collapsible mountage, mulberry twig, paddy straw, grasses etc., are kept on the rearing bed directly. Cocooning frames are left for 4-6 hrs and mature larvae are allowed to crawl up on to the mountages due to its negative geotropic nature. This process is repeated twice. When more than 80 per cent larvae crawled up, mountages are removed and placed separately. If few larvae are still left in the rearing bed, they are hand picked and mounted on mounting frames. However, in this method, silkworm waste lot of silk and floss percentage increases.

Chemical for Uniform Maturity

Central Sericultural Research and Training Institute, Mysore has developed a commercial plant product known as 'Sampoorna' which accelerate the maturation process. Sampoorna is a spinning hormone of plant origin which contains ß-ecdysone. The spraying od sampoorna is carried out when first symptoms of spinning is observed during 5th instar. Spraying is 0.2 per cent sampoorna is carried out @ one liter/10000 larvae uniformly. For the purpose one ample (20 ml) of sampoorna is mixed with one liter of cleaned water in a container to prepare 0.2 per cent solution for spraying on the leaf. The leaf is cut into small pieces and solution is sprayed on the leaf and mixed properly. This leaf is given as light but last feed to the silkworm. After few hours when matured larvae starts spinning, mountages are placed over them or larvae are picked and transferred on the mountages depending on the type of mountages used and method of mounting. The advantage of use of sampoorna includes –

- Accelerates the process of maturation of larvae for spinning without affecting quality of cocoons and cocoon yield.
- It reduces mounting period by 18-40 hrs.
- As all the larvae matured within a day, the manpower to be utilised in plucking of leaf, bed cleaning etc., can be saved.
- The silkworm crops can be saved from shortage of leaf if any during last instar when large quantity of leaf is required for feeding and also from the occurrence of diseases if any.

Mounting Density

Mounting of mature silkworm larvae per unit area plays an important role in determining the cocoon production quality, inspite of healthy larvae are mounted. In India maximum used mountages are bamboo made chandrikee followed by collapsible plastic mountages. The density of larvae to be mounted on the types of mountages used for mounting purpose.

- About 40-50 mature silkworm larvae can be mounted per square feet area in bamboo made chandrikee and collapsible plastic mountages.
- About 450-500 mature silkworm larvae can be mounted in bottle brushed mountages of one meter length.
- Rotary card board mountages has 1560 cubicles but 80 per cent of it *i.e.*, 1200 mature silkworm larvae are mounted.
- Bamboo spiral round mounatges (dalla) has capacity to accommodate 300-400 mature silkworm larvae depending on the size of the tray (3 or 4 feet diameter).

If mature silkworm larvae are mounted more than the optimum number, defective cocoon percentage will be increased and cocoon quality will be inferior and if the number is less than the optimum, number of cocooning frames require will be more which becomes laborious, uneconomical and also require more space for mounting.

Causes of Non-spinning Silkworms

(a) *Caused by Chemicals:* Traces of chemicals when comes in contact with larvae during rearing makes the central nervous system of silkworm paralyze and affects its normal spinning, resulting non-spinning silkworms. This case is more serious when such contact is during the later stage of 4th instar.

(b) *Caused by Diseases:* Silkworm diseases like Grassarie, Flacharie, Muscardine and Pebrine etc., also cause non-spinning of silkworms.

(c) *Physiological Causes:* The non-spinning/cocooning silkworms may be caused by overgrown silk glands which suppresses the tracheae at the border of head and thorax of the larvae or by in-coordination between the spinning movement and dehydration of liquid sericin which affects the liquid silk to become silk wave or by the abnormal distribution of tracheae on the posterior silk gland, which hinders the gland and normal activity of breath or sometimes it may be caused by malformation of silk gland cells in the middle or posterior part of the gland.

(d) *Unfavourable Environment:* Unfavorable environment during rearing *viz;* too high rearing temperature or too tender leaves makes imbalance in the endocrine system resulting in the abnormal development of silk gland. Harmful gases during rearing also cause non-cocooning of silkworms. High temperature and high humidity during mounting affects respiratory rate of mature silkworm larvae leading to physiological abnormality and paralyzed nerves, whereas, low temperature during mounting may prolong the cocooning period and in these both cases induce non-cocooning silkworms.

(e) *Improper Handling:* Improper handling during mounting sometimes injure the silkworms body wall or silk gland etc., and makes the larvae unable to form cocoon.

Defective Cocoons

The cocoons which are not suitable for reeling or difficult to reel are known as defective cocoons. Inadequate mounting care, poor hygienic conditions during spinning, use of poor quality of mountages, pests and diseases etc., meads to formation of defective cocoons. The defective cocoons are broadly classified into the following categories –

(a) *Immature Cocoons:* Immature cocoons are those, where the pupal formation is incomplete. This occurs usually when cocoons are harvested prematurely. Therefore, to avoid occurrence of immature cocoons, harvesting should be performed when pupa appears dark brown in colour, slightly shrunken in size with glistering eyes.

(b) *Rusty Cocoons*: In some cases, intestinal fluid of matured larvae during spinning in mountages falls on already-formed cocoons. Such cocoons produce rustling sound when shaken individually, indicating sticking of dead papa to the sides of the shell. Such putrefying pupae stain the shell and make it unfit for reeling.

(c) *Black Stained Cocoons:* Due to putrification of pupae, black stains appears on the outside of cocoons and thus spoiling them and making them unfit for ommercial reeling. Such cocoons must promptly be removed from the healthy lot to avoid spoiling of it.

(d) *Spotted Cocoons:* Improper storage of cocoons under bad ventilation and damp condition causes development of a fungus belonging to the family *Aspergillaceae* on the shell leading to brownish or yellow spot on the cocoons, deteriorating its quality.

(e) *Weak-end Cocoons:* Weak-end cocoons are formed due to unfavorable environmental conditions during spinning besides due to use of improper mountages. Weak-end cocoons are invariably formed in multivoltine breeds.

(f) *Malformed Cocoons:* Overcrowding at the time of spinning and use of bad mountages lead to malformed/deformed cocoons. These cocoons are abnormal in shape, scaffold-pressed or cocoons having non-uniform texture of cocoon shell rendering them unfit for commercial reeling. Such cocoons appear when a number of irregular spaces occur in cocooning frame or when larvae are not healthy.

(g) *Calcified Cocoons:* In these types of cocoons, pupae are destroyed due to attack of fungus called *Botrytis bassina.*

(h) *Loose-knit/fragile Cocoons:* Loosely built with open space between layers constituting the shell form knit/fragile cocoons.

(i) *Undersized Cocoons:* These cocoons are below normal in size with thin cocoon shell and very low cocoon-shell ratio. These cocoons should not be reeled properly.

(j) *Mutes Cocoons:* Pupa becomes dead and sticks to the shell inside the cocoon and hence does not make any sound when shaken. Decaying pupa sometimes releases putrefying body fluid, which stains the cocoon-shell.

(k) *Double Cocoons:* One pupa per cocoon is a regular/universal phenomenon in silk insects. The metamorphosis of two larvae and rarely three, into pupa, in one and the same cocoon is referred as double cocoon formation. The double cocoons are also called jointed cocoons/combined cocoons or associated cocoons. Various factors are responsible for the formation of double cocoons, which includes types of mountages used, density of spinning larvae, silkworm breed and mounting care. These double cocoons are abnormally shaped and thick-shelled cocoons. They can not be reeled to get uniform yarn. As it is not a genetic character, these types of cocoons can be used in seed production. Double cocoons are mostly used to produce dupion silk.

(l) *Pierced Cocoons:* Due to Uzi infection, the Uzi maggots penetrate the cocoon shell and makes hole to come out of the cocoon to pupate. These are pierced cocoons which are unfit for reeling to get continuous filament.

(m) *Printed Cocoons:* While cocooning, some part of the cocoon surface adhered to the cocooning surface imprinted by the latter. Even if it is small, raw silk can not be reeled from such cocoons. This problem occurs when the material used for making the mountages are too hard or cocooning space is too small.

Causes of Defective Cocoons

Defective cocoons should not exceed 5-10 per cent of the total cocoons harvested from a batch if mature silkworms are picked up timely and good mountages and proper mounting methods are followed. However, sometimes it exceeds above 15 per cent affecting reeling performance, leading to higher renditta and economic loss to reeler. The defective cocoons fetch low price. The defective cocoons are formed due to –

- High humidity and lack of proper ventilation in the mounting establishments.
- Overcrowding of mature silkworm larvae per unit area in the mountages.
- Improper maintenance of hygienic conditions during rearing.
- Use of bad quality of mountages.
- High temperature and humidity during rearing of late instar larvae.

- Secondary contamination at the final stage of silkworm rearing.

To reduce occurrence of such non-reelable cocoons, the following care must be taken –

- Mature worms should be mounted as early as possible.
- Simple, eco-friendly and easy to handle mountages should be chosen which avoids crowding of larvae.
- Optimum temperature, humidity and air current should be maintained in the mounting room and keeps the mountages away from direct sunlight and strong wind.
- Harvesting of cocoons must be done after completion of pupation.
- Care should be taken during cocoon transportation and storage.

The type and nature of mountages, mounting technology and spinning conditions play a vital role in the production of quality cocoons. Correct time of mounting of mature larvae and harvesting of cocoons after proper pupation is very important to minimize the defective cocoons. Even after raising healthy and robust silkworms, incorrect mounting technology and use of improper type of mountages can lead to formation of inferior types of cocoons.

CHAPTER

8

Cocoon Harvest and Transport

Silk material have received much attention in recent years because of their attractive combinations of mechanical strength and toughness as well as environmentally benign conditions under which materials are processed from concentrated protein solutions to solid fibres (Porter and Vollrath, 2009). However, silkworm cocoons which are best known as the main commercial source of silk material are themselves remarkable material. A cocoon is a natural silk composite with a non-woven structure made of continuous silk fibres conglutinated by sericin binding matrix (Chen *et al.* 2012). As a biological structural material, it has a hierarchical structure that has been optimized through evolutionary pressures over millions of years to provide the optimum protection for the silkworm pupae, as they transforms into moth and are exposed to wide range of threats such as physical attack from animals, birds or insects and more subtle threats such as bacteria or harsh environment (Chen *et al.* 2012).

Of the many contributing factors responsible for the production of quality cocoons, rearing and mounting environment, type of mountages used, rearing season and racial characteristic of the breed/hybrid plays a major role. Silk gland is the source of silk. Silk gland is transformed labial gland having three distinct and functional parts – *(i)* the posterior, *(ii)* the middle and *(iii)* the anterior with 500, 250 and 300 gland cells respectively at each side with approximately 2000 gland cells altogether. It increases 1.6×10^5 fold from hatching to full grown larvae without any cell division. During the growth of larvae, it increases 20, 6, 5 and 40 folds in different instars larvae and finally accounts for 40 per cent of the larval body weight. Posterior part secretes silk substance known as 'fibroin', while the middle part serves as reservoir for receiving the fibroin from the posterior silk gland. It also secretes around the fibroin, a natural gummy substance known as 'sericin'. These substances when coming into contact with air harden into silk filament. Posterior end of the gland is closed while fore end joins together to a common excretory duct opening into the spinneret. Silkworm cocooning process may be divided into four stages as shown below –

1. Mature silkworm that appears translucent raises its head and crawls here and there to find a suitable cocooning site. It first spins some silk waves into the mounting to form a framework of a cocoon and then continues to spin to form a cocoon net. Irregular and loose silk is spun to thicken the cocoon net and gradually cocoon frame is formed.
2. The worms body bends towards its back, its abdominal legs are fixed on the internal wall of the cocoon cavity, its head swings left and right to spin silk.
3. Secretion of large quantity of silk makes the silkworm shrink remarkably. The swinging of its head slows down and finally loses the rhythm of swinging. As a result, a thin layer of pupal covering is formed. Finally, towards the upper end of the cocoon, larva secretes the last silk material forming a loose and soft cocoon top. Thus, the cocooning process is completed and the larva becomes ready for pupation. High quality cocoons should be firm and compact in built, uniform in size and shape, rich in

silk content with minimal floss. For international market grade 'A' cocoon should have average shell weight of 0.40 gm or above and anything below 0.40 gm is considered lacking in quality for 'A' grade silk and does not attract buyers to purchase at higher rate.

If the temperature rises beyond 22-25^{0}C during spinning, the shell becomes very loose and folded with wrinkles and knot (Rahmathulla, 2012). It also changes the properties of sericin. Low temperature slows down the secretion of silk thread, resulting in large sized cocoons. Relative humidity of 60-70 per cent induces good health, good reelability and good quality cocoons.

Cocoon Harvest

After spinning the cocoon, larvae under goes metamorphosis inside the cocoon and becomes pupa. Generally pupation takes 4-5 days after spinning in Bivoltine and 3-4 days in multivoltine. The pupa when formed has thin cuticular skin which is soft and ruptures easily if disturbed and therefore early harvesting of cocoons should be avoided. The appropriate time for harvesting of cocoon varies according to the prevailing environment conditions (Rajan *et al.* 1997). In hot areas, harvesting is carried out earlier than in cold areas. Under ideal conditions, Bivoltine cocoons are harvested on 7th day of mounting. In very hot areas they can be harvested before 5th or 6th day while in cold places it may take as many as ten days or more before harvesting. The proper time for harvesting of cocoons is when the pupae appear dark brown in colour, hard and cocoon shell is dry. In this form it is suitable for long distance transportation for marketing. This usually occurs on the sixth or seventh day after mounting. Early harvesting is not good as it leads to harvesting premature pupae leading to less price of the cocoon. Delay in harvesting is also disadvantageous to the sericulture farmers because the cocoons will lose weight due to the continuous evaporation of the body fluids from the pupae while transforming into adult for emergence and also the cocoon buyer/reeler will not get sufficient time for proper stifling of cocoons before storage or reeling. At the time of cocoon harvest farmer must first remove the diseased or dead silkworms and spoiled cocoons from the mountages as they tend to stain good cocoons affecting their quality. While harvesting, care should be taken to remove the bad cocoons. These include double cocoons, stained cocoons, thin shelled cocoons and deformed cocoons. It is also necessary to remove the excessive floss and all other loosely sticking dirt such as silkworm litter and bits of mulberry leaves from the cocoons.

Cocoons may also stick to one another and make the handling process difficult. Excessive floss can be removed by farmers themselves, using simple devices like iron rods before they are taken to the cocoon market. Under no circumstances fresh cocoons are piled up after harvesting. Piling up does not only make respiration of pupae difficult but also heat and moisture will form and spoil the cocoon quality. Cocoons should be spread in a thin layer on a clean polythene sheet or mat. They should not be put into bags where they may stay for several hours. Bags should only be used when transporting them to the cocoon market. Cocoons should be taken to the cocoon market immediately after harvesting as prolonged storage may lead to the pupae developing into moths. Cocoons must be graded according to grades of quality. In some states as there is no cocoon market, sericulture farmers are forced to dry the cocoons after harvest and sold when buyers when they come for the purchase. Drying should be done perfectly in the cocoon drying chamber. If no drying chamber is available nearby, they can be dried up in the sun light. These dried cocoons can be stored for some time. However, long storage of cocoons at farmers' establishments is not advisable as it leads to deterioration in the quality besides damage of cocoons by rats, ants, dermestid beetles etc.

Physical and Commercial Characteristics of Cocoon

The cocoon filament is a typical protein fiber consisting of two filaments of fibroin cemented with sericin besides other matters such as wax, fatty acids, inorganic matters and colours. The major components are –

Fibroin	:	70-80%
Sericin	:	18-28%
Carbohydrates	:	1.2-1.6%
Fat and Wax	:	0.5-1.0%
Colouring matter and minerals	:	1.0-1.4%

The pH of fibroin is 2.1-2.5, having a chemical formula of C15 H26 N5 O6, while sericin has a pH of 3.8-4.2 with a chemical formula of C15 H25 N5 O6. Sericin and fibroin content of the cocoon filament appears to be dependent on the silkworm breeds/hybrids. The sericin content in multivoltine is more compared to Bivoltine silk by about 2-4 per cent. Since the percentage of sericin content is very important from the commercial point of view, weavers prefer less sericin in the raw silk purchased.

Colour

Cocoon colour is racial characteristics. It is due to the presence of carotenoid or flavanoid pigments in the sericin layer. Universally cocoons are of two colors *viz;* white and yellow. White colour can further be divided into pure white, grayish white and silver white. The yellow colour can further be divided into golden yellow, orange yellow, brown yellow, greenish yellow etc. The colour does not influence reeling parameters and is also not permanent as it washes away with the sericin during the degumming process. Moreover, generally reeling industry prefers white cocoons as the raw material and thus most of the silk growing countries raise white Bivoltine cocoons.

Cocoon Grains

The cocoon shell has granular surface wrinkled with convolutions is known as cocoon wrinkles or grains. Wrinkles are coarser on the outer layer and are very clear and gradually get reduced towards the inner shell till almost they disappear at the inner most layer of the shell. In general, if the wrinkles are even and light, the elasticity of the cocoon shell is good. It is generally recognised that coarse wrinkled cocoons reel poorly.

Cocoon Luster

Cocoon luster is linked to cocoon colour and degree of permeability of the shell to light and light reflection capacity. In general, if cocoon shell is thick, light rays cannot penetrate it easily and hence luster is comparatively less. Cocoon with thin shell layer can easily passage of light rays and therefore reflection is uniform causing good luster. White colour cocoons have strong light reflection capacity and so have comparatively better luster. To get better luster it is important to maintain mounting micro-environment at the optimum level of temperature, humidity and air circulation, besides only ripened larvae should be pickup and mounted for spinning and to provide proper spacing of larvae in the mountage.

Size

Cocoon size or volume is a critical characteristic for evaluating cocoon characteristics. The size of the cocoon varies from breed to breed, season to season, rearing practices adopted, spacing between larvae during rearing and mounting. The number of cocoons per liter usually indicates the size of cocoon. The number of cocoons per liter in Bivoltine breeds varies between 60 and 90 while in multivoltine it measures more considerably.

Shape

The cocoon shape is racial character and one of the important parameter for differentiating different breeds and evaluating reelability. The shape of the cocoon can be classified as round, oval, oblong, constricted, elliptical, spherical, pointed end, peanut shape etc. Hybrid cocoons assume a shape midway between the parents. Further, the shape can be affected by the execution of the mounting process especially during the cocoon spinning stage. Cocoons which show slight constriction and the ones with oval shape are the best for automatic reeling machines. Cocoons having too deep constriction in the middle or with very noticeable points are not suitable for steady reeling. These contain a comparatively shorter length of silk filament, easily break and thus interrupt steady reeling and increase wastage of silk. Cocoon uniformity in size/shape and build are a guiding principle in predetermining or forecasting the quality of raw silk filament, nature of the cocoons and percentage of the silk in the cocoons. In order to enhance uniformity, rearing and mounting management have to be done on scientific basis. Cocoon uniformity of 85 per cent and above is considered as good and less than 75 per cent as bad and between 75-85 per cent as ordinary.

Cocoon Weight

It is very important from the point of view of reeling. Cocoon weight is racial character but varies with season to season; rearing method adopted; quality and quantity of mulberry leaf fed etc. Female cocoon is heavier than the male cocoons. Prices are paid on the basis of weight. If the cocoons are small in size but their weight is relatively satisfactory, this indicates that the quality of silk contained in them is good. With this, one can determine the 'Renditta', which is the quantity of cocoon required to produce one unit of raw silk. From a good lot reared the average cocoon weight should range between 1.8 gm and 2.0 gm. In nature, the weight of a fresh cocoon does not remain constant but instead continues to decrease until the pupae transforms into adult and emerges from the cocoon. This weight decrease occurs gradually as moisture evaporates from the body of the pupae and fat is consumed during the metamorphosis process. Therefore, farmer should sell cocoon on 6th or 7th day of mounting/2nd or 3rd day of pupation otherwise with reduction in weight of cocoon, the farmers will be in loss as more cocoon will be required for the same unit weight.

Shell Weight

The weight of the silk shell is the most consequential factor as this measure forecasts raw silk yield. Shell weight is also a racial character and varies from breed to breed, season to season, leaf quality fed to silkworm, technology used for rearing and mounting and frequency of feeding during silkworm rearing. High cocoon shell weight is an important trait for high productivity. Generally, Univoltine and Bivoltine genotypes produce heavier shell weights than multivoltine species. From a good lot reared, the average shell weight should be above 0.40 gm.

Hardness or Compactness

This represents the levels of stiffness and elasticity. If the cocoon shell is pressed with a finger and felt stiff and elastic, it is called the compact and when it is loose and non-elastic is called loose. Cocoon compactness is dependent on shell texture and is affected by cocoon spinning conditions. If during the mounting process, humidity is low it causes cocoon layer soft, while high humidity makes it hard. The degree of hardness also influences air and water permeability of cocoons during boiling. A hard shell typically reduces reelability (during the cocoon reeling process), while a soft-shell may multiply raw silk defects. In short, moderate humidity is preferred for good quality cocoons. In general, when the cocoon is pressed with fingers its thickness should be even and elasticity should be appropriate for proper cocoon reeling. Further, it is also established that the anterior region (head region) and middle region (central constricted part) of the cocoon shell is more compact than the posterior region (tail region) of the cocoon (Table 8.1)

Table 8.1: Variation in Shell Thickness in Different Parts

Breed		Breed 'A'		Breed 'B'		Breed 'C'	
Head (anterior part)	Shell Region	Micron	Index	Micron	Index	Micron	Index
	Extreme End	336	47	302	43	228	40
	Expanded End	564	83	596	85	480	84
Central constricted		712	100	700	100	572	100
Tail (posterior part)	Extreme End	568	80	590	84	466	81
	Expanded End	382	54	333	48	348	43

Shell Percentage

The weight of the silk filament is decided by the weight of the cocoon and shell. As the entire cocoon including the pupa is sold as part of the raw material, it is essential to quantify the ratio of the weight of the silk shell versus the weight of the cocoon. These values is obtained by dividing the weight of single cocoon shell by weight of single cocoon and multiply by 100 as indicated below –

$$\text{Shell \%} = \frac{\text{Shell weight (gm)}}{\text{Cocoon weight (gm)}} \times 100$$

This value gives a satisfactory indication of the amount of raw silk that can be reeled from a given quantity of fresh cocoons under transaction. The calculation assists in estimating the raw silk yield of the cocoon and in deriving an appropriate price for the cocoons. The percentage will change based on the breed of the silkworms, environmental conditions, quantity of mulberry leaf fed, rearing technology adopted, type of mountages used and mounting conditions. Percentage rates are also dependent on the age of the cocoons as the pupa loses weight as metamorphosis continues. It is advantageous to have shell ratio of about 21-23 per cent, where male cocoons have higher shell ratio than female cocoons. It is reported that silkworm breeds with higher cocoon shell ratio have less resistance to diseases compared to those with less shell ratio. Therefore, effort should be made to balance between shell ratio and resistance of silkworm breeds to diseases.

Raw Silk Percentage

Silk as reeled from cocoon is known as raw silk. It contains its original gum or sericin. Raw silk percentage calculation is the most important for the value of the cocoon as it has a direct impact on both the market price of cocoons and the production costs of raw silk. The normal range is 65-84 per cent for the weight of the cocoon shell and 12-20 per cent for the weight of the whole fresh cocoon.

Specific Gravity of Silk

The specific gravity on an average of sericin and fibroin varies between 1.32-1.40 (Table 8.2). Generally, the specific gravity of sericin is slightly higher than of fibroin.

Table 8.2: Specific Gravity and Tensile Strength of Various Fibres

Fibres	Specific Gravity	Tenacity (g/denier)	Elongation
Raw silk	1.32-1.40	2.60-4.80	18-23
Degummed silk	1.30-1.38	–	–
Wool	1.30-1.40	1.20-1.50	30-48
Cotton	1.52-1.60	3.20-4.80	7-11
Flax	1.50-1.58	4.80-6.00	2-4
Nylon	1.14-1.17	4.50-5.00	25-30

Filament Length

The length of filament contained in the cocoon shell is as important as shell ratio. This is measured by reeling silk thread from single cocoon. The length of filament depends on the quality of cocoons, voltinism of silkworm (Univoltine, Bivoltine or Multivoltine or their hybrids). In general, the total filament length of a cocoon is around 400-600 meter in multivoltine breeds and 700-1500 meter in bivoltine.

Reelability

The reelability is the most important character that influences raw silk yield, productivity and raw silk quality. Reelability is defined as the fitness of cocoon for economically feasible reeling. Poor reelability does not only cause stoppage in production but also results in increase in wastage. Reelability of cocoon is influenced by care taken during spinning of silkworm larvae, prevailing temperature and humidity during cocooning stage, drying, storage, operational skill etc. Therefore, effort should be taken to maintain required temperature and humidity during spinning and the spinning larvae should not be disturbed.

Sorting of Cocoon

After the cocoons are harvested from the cocooning frame, the defective cocoons are to be sorted out to get the good price and more profit. For this purpose defective cocoons *viz;* double cocoons, stained cocoons, flimsy cocoons, thin end cocoons, pierced cocoons, melted cocoons etc., are sorted out before transacting the cocoons in the cocoon market. This improves the reeling performance and recovery of quality silk.

Floss Removal

Cocoon shell has three distinctive layers. The outer layer (floss or blaze), the middle compact layer (reelable silk), and inner most (pelade) layer. The outer layer (floss/blaze) and inner most layers (pelade) are not reelable and form the waste. The floss is the foundation layer of the cocoon shell which covers the middle compact reelable part of the shell. Thus, after harvesting of cocoons from the mountages, the floss have to be removed before its utilisation for seed production or commercial reeling. The process of floss removal from the cocoon shell is known as deflossing or peeling. The floss percentage in respect to shell weight in multivoltine forms is 10-12 per cent, Bivoltine: 7-9 per cent and multi x Bivoltine: 4-6 per cent (Samson *et al.* 1994). The floss percentage of some popular multivoltine genotypes is presented in Table 8.3. In evolved multivoltine genotypes, floss percentage is less in comparison to traditional indigenous genotypes. It is highest in Pure Mysore genotype (18.4%) which is flossier with weak cocoon shell layer.

Table 8.3: Floss (%) in Some Multivoltine Genotypes (Samson *et al.* 1994)

Improved Genotypes	Floss %	Indigenous Genotypes	Floss (%)
Mysore Princes	7.2	Nistari	9.2
Hosa Mysore	6.4	Tamil Nadu (W)	10.4
Killegal Jawan	5.9	Moria	11.6
Kolar Gold	6.8	Sarupat	12.0
MW1	7.2	Pure Mysore	18.4
MW2	5.3		
G	7.4		
C. Nichi	6.6		

Importance of Deflossing

- Deflossing is essential to judge the quality of cocoon.
- The correct shape, size, volume and grain of cocoons are practically possible only after deflossing.
- Floss absorbs moisture from the nature leading to deterioration of the quality of cocoon.
- Intact cocoon with floss creates inconvenience in handling because floss of cocoons gets stuck to each other.
- Intact cocoon with floss obstruct easy flow of cocoons in the automatic reeling machine leading to slow processing.
- Cocoon with floss require more labour and time during reeling operation besides increasing wastage of the material.
- Colour of the cocoon becomes brighter after deflossing because dirt and dust accumulated during spinning and harvesting are removed.
- Reelability improves after deflossing of cocoon.
- Deflossed cocoons can be stored in a unit area in comparison to un-deflossed cocoons.
- Dry floss fetches highest price among all the variety of silk waste as it is used for the production of spun silk yarn.
- Dry floss can conveniently be used as filing material in pillows and beddings.
- Dry floss can also be used fore knitting of winter jacket and gloves.

Methods of Deflossing

There are two principle methods of deflossing. They are hand deflossing and machine deflossing.

(i) Hand Deflossing

If the quantity of cocoon is less or cocoon-shell is weak, the deflossing is done by hand. Multivoltine cocoons which are generally weak having thin cocoon shell layer are subjected to deflossing by shorter themselves. In this process floss from each individual is removed by peeling them with the help of fingers. As each and every cocoon have to be passed through the fingers of the sorters, only desired quantity of floss can be removed. Though, it is most efficient method of deflossing, yet it consumes lot of time and labour hence, it is advisable only when the sample quantity is less. Invariably, this system is adopted by breeders and also by the seed producers. Moreover, it is not practicable for commercial reeling because hardly 1.2 kg of cocoon can be deflossed in an hour by the sorer.

Hand deflossing is also carried out with the use of rod. An iron rod of 1.00 cm thickness and 2.0 feet in length having slight rough surface is used in this system. One end of this rod is bent into a handle. This rod is fixed with the help of clamps on some wooden platform. It is fixed in such a way, that it facilitates easy movement of cocoons from the lower and upper surface of the rod. The rod for use is moistening with a wet cloth. A heap of cocoon is put on this rod for the purpose of deflossing. The deflosser holds loosely the handle end and turns it skillfully and briskly. The moisten rod while moving collects the floss around itself. The heap of cocoon is given periodic turnings by hand to ensure uniform deflossing. Only 2.0 kg cocoons can be deflossed at a time. By this system, one person can defloss 4-5 kg of cocoons. But this system is not very efficient because only 40-50 per cent of floss can be removed from the cocoons. Hence again deflossing of cocoon is necessary to get better results. This system can be used for deflossing hybrid cocoons and Bivoltine cocoons because of compact shell layers.

(ii) Machine Deflossing

Cocoons of Bivoltine and their hybrids are naturally firm built having compact shell layers and less floss. These cocoons can conveniently be utilised for deflossing by machine. Usually the machines used for the purpose are either hand or power driven deflossers. Reeling sectors mostly use power driven deflosser for deflossing purpose. This type of machine can defloss 10-12 kg of cocoons/hr with the deflossing efficiency of 95 per cent. The cocoons which are weak and this cocoon shell layers are crushed in this process creating obstruction in deflossing. Therefore, this system can be used only for those cocoons which have firm built besides compact cocoon shell layer.

The hand driven deflosser is most convenient method as it is driven manually. This type of deflosser is suitable for Bivoltine and cross breed cocoons deflossing only. Approximately, 8-10 kg of cocoons with 70 per cent efficiency can be deflossed by this system in an hour. The cocoon deflossing efficiency of different deflossing system (Mishra, 1989) is presented in Table 8.4.

Table 8.4: Cocoon Deflossing Efficiency of Different Deflossing Systems

Deflossing System	Voltinism/ Combination	Cocoon Defloss/ hr (kg.)	Deflossing Efficiency (%)
Common Hand Deflossing	Multivoltine, Multi x Bi, Bivoltine, Univoltine	1-2	100
Hand deflossing with rod	Multi x Bi, Bivoltine, Univoltine	4-6	40
Hand driven deflossing machine	Bivoltine, Univoltine	8-10	70
Power driven deflossing machine	Bivoltine, Univoltine	10-12	95

Cocoon Drying

The objective of drying are to kill pupae in order to prevent the pupa transforming into moth and coming out of the cocoons by piercing them. Once the cocoons are pierced, they are not useful for reeling as the continuity of filament is broken. There are three methods in practice for drying of green cocoons *viz*; steam stifling, sun drying and hot air drying. Steam stifling kills' pupae but unable to remove the moisture and therefore storage of steam stifled cocoon is not possible as they will be prone to fungus attack. In Sun drying, both stifling and drying of cocoons is carried out together, but exposes cocoons to ultra violet rays, which affect the reelability and turns silk yellow. However, farmers are mostly left with no choice but to go for sun drying as other facility availability is too far from their reach. Hot air drying is most suitable method to stifle the cocoons for reeling quality silk.

In sun drying method, cocoons are exposed to the scorching action of direct sun light till the pupa inside is killed and dried. The sun dried cocoons are very light and produces a rattling sound on shaking. This method is very cheap and easy and dried cocoons can be stored for any length of time. However, the sunlight should be of sufficient intensity and duration for proper drying of cocoons which is not uniform in all the seasons and regions. Further, prolonged exposure to sunlight adversely affects the quality of silk and increases the proportion of silk waste during reeling. In steam drying method wet steam is used. By this method, cocoons are dried very quickly and uniformly. However, in this method only pupa is killed inside but it is not dried. The best method considered now-a-days for drying of cocoons is batch type hot air dryers or ushnakoti. In this method, the drying chamber is heated up to 120°C and cocoons are put inside it. The cocoons are initially heated up to remove the moisture mixed in the air inside the cocoon at a faster rate so that sericin in the inner layer is not affected. In its inner layer, the cocoons are dried using the temperature profile as in Table 8.5 (Datta and Nanavaty, 2007).

Table 8.5: Temperature Profile for Air Drying Cocoons

Temperature (°C)	Duration (in hour)
115-120°C	1
100°C	1
85°C	1
70°C	1
55°C	1

Optimum Degree of Drying

The optimum degree of drying can be calculated by the following formula –

$$\text{Degree of drying (\%)} = \frac{\text{Dry weight of cocoons}}{\text{Green weight of cocoons}} \times 100$$

If the cocoons are not dried to the optimum level, they are again dried at lower temperature (98^0-60^0C). Optimum degree of drying can be calculated on the basis of shell ratio of cocoon lots using the following formula –

$$\text{Optimum degree of drying} = \frac{\text{100 \% Shell Ratio (\%)}}{4} + \text{Shell ratio}$$

Packing of Cocoons

After sorting of cocoons and its floss removal, the cocoons are spread on plastic mat in a single layer till marketing. Good cocoons can be packed in perforated gunny or plastic bags loosely and transported to cocoon market during cooler hours of the day. However, there will be emergence after 8-10 days of spinning and therefore if marketing is delayed, cocoons should be dried and kept for marketing packed in perforated gunny bags or plastic bags.

Storage of Cocoons

Dried cocoons are stored for varying periods by farmers as well as by reeling units. During storage, they may be damaged either by the beetles, *Dermestus,* rodents or by fungal growth (Harishchandra *et al.* 1999).

Dermestid Beetle

Grubs and adults of dermestid beetle make hole in the cocoon, enter inside and eat the dried pupae. They also damage pierced and melted cocoons. The damage level estimated by Thiagarajan and Govindaiah (1987) due to the beetle attack to the pupae of silkworm is 16.62 per cent and moth 3.57 per cent with total loss of 20.19 per cent in Government grainages in Karnataka. The list of demestid beetle damaging stored cocoons and their products in different countries is presented in Table 8.6 (Vijayaveer *et al.* 1996).

Table 8.6: **Dermestid Insect Pests of Stored Silkworm Cocoons and their Products**

Species	Commodity Damaged	Country
Thylodrius contractus	Silk fabrics	USA
Dermestes alter	Cocoons, Raw silk	Germany, India, USA, Japan
D. coarctatus	Eggs, Cocoons, Silk	Japan
D. frischii	Cocoons, raw silk	Italy, Central Asia
D. lardarius	Cocoons, Eggs, Caterpillars	Bulgaria, France, Italy
D. leechi	Cocoons	India
D. maculates	Moth, Raw silk	Italy, India
D. murinus	Cocoons, Raw silk	Italy
D. peruvianus	Raw silk	Britain
D. tesclataocollis	Raw silk	India
D. undulates	Cocoons, Raw silk	Central Asia, India
D. vorax	Cocoons, Raw silk	India
Attagenus fasciatus	Cocoons, Fabrics	India
A. birmanicus	Cocoons	India
A. pellio	Cocoons	Germany, Georgia
A. unicolor	Cocoons, Fabrics	USSR, North America
A. unicolor japonicus	Cocoons, Raw silk, Floss, Fabrics	Japan
Trogoderma sternale	Cocoons, Raw silk	USA
T. halsteadi	Cocoons	India
T. varium	Cocoons, Eggs, Raw silk	Japan
T. versicolor	Cocoons, Raw silk	Georgia, Central Asia
Orphinus fulvipes	Cocoons	India
Anthrenus flavipes	Cocoons, Fabrics	Africa, India, Germany
A. museorum	Silk	Germany
A. pimpinellae	Cocoons	India
A. scrophularae	Silk	North America
A. verbasci	Cocoons, Raw silk, Fabrics,	Canada, Italy, Japan, USA
Trnodes rufesceens	Cocoons, Raw silk	Japan

The following precautions must be taken against dermestid beetle –

- Cocoons must be dried completely.
- Cocoons must be stored in rooms with good ventilation so that humidity inside the storage room is maintained below 70 per cent.
- Cocoons must be inspected and turned frequently so that they have good aeration.
- Stained or mould attacked cocoons if any should be removed carefully as soon as observed.
- Avoid longer storage of rejected/pierced cocoons.
- Collect the grubs and adults either by sweeping or using a vacuum cleaner and destroy them by burning or dipping in soap water.
- Proper disinfections of cocoon storage room besides periodical cleaning.
- Provide a wire mesh to the doors and windows of pierced cocoon storage rooms to avoid entry of the beetles and grubs.
- Fumigate dried cocoon (not live) storage room with methyl bromide or with chloropicrin.
- Pierced cocoons should be stored in deltamethrin treated bags (soak the bags in 0.028% deltamethrin solution and dry in shade).
- Spray 0.028 per cent deltamethrin solution on walls and floor of pierced cocoon (PC) storage room once in three months.
- Sprinkle bleaching powder (200 gm/m^2) all around inner wall of PC storage room to prevent crawling of grubs from PC room.

Rodents

They constitute the largest order of existing mammals. Management of rodents is a very intricate as well as a ticklish problem. Rodents infest an area throughout the year as compared to other pests which appear sporadically only for short period in certain seasons (Reddy *et al.* 1989). Rodents continue to damage stored cocoons. The Lesser Bandicoot or field rat (*Bandicota bengalensis*), grass rat (*Millardia meltada*), Indian field mouse (*Mus booduga*), common rat (*Rattus rattus*), gerbil rat (*Tatera indica*), common house rat (*Rattus rattus rufescens*) are important pests damaging stored cocoons in India. The poisons used for the control of rodents are either acute poisons (single dose and quick acting) or chronic poison (multiple dose and slow acting). A rodenticide must have three ideal attributes – *(i)* toxicity, *(ii)* acceptability and *(iii)* safety in use. The acute poisons are better for giving a quick knock down, but they have little selectivity and poor efficacy. They require pre-baiting, as rodents develop bait shyness for them. Anticoagulants have advantage as far as efficacy and safety are concerned, but are slow in action, more laborious and hence the treatment cost is comparatively higher. However, the best method is trapping. The traps may of live traps, kill types traps. Rodents can also be prevented by putting wire mesh on all the windows, and providing hedges around the cocoon storage room.

Transportation and Marketing of Cocoons

After proper harvesting and removal of diseased or damaged cocoons, the cocoons are taken to the market for sale. For short distances farmers transport the cocoons in bamboo basket, jute bags, gunny bags or plastic bags on their head or on by-cycle. If the distance of cocoon market is longer, the cocoons are transported in van or a bus. Caution should be exercised when green cocoons are transported. Vibration and shock during long distance may spoil green cocoons. Also, the container in which green cocoons are to be transported to be loosely packed in vans. It is advisable to avoid transport green cocoons to long distances. To minimize the risk of damage to be caused due to heat generated, it is suggested to transport the cocoons during cooler hours of the day *i.e.*, either during night or in the early morning.

For any agricultural or industrial produce, good and timely marketing linkage serves as a boon to growers who get motivated to take up such activities. More so due to quality concern, shown by the prospective buyers, a sense of responsiveness is generated among the farmers who exercise utmost care during rearing and attempt to produce quality cocoons, which fetches good returns (Baqual *et al.* 2013). The economic value of reeling and the quality of reeled product depends largely on the quality of cocoons. The price of cocoons in the market is decided on the basis of its quality (Table 8.7).

Table 8.7: Cocoon Pricing by Individual Inspection

Shell %	Good Cocoons %	Fictitious Raw Silk % of Fresh Cocoons	Grade
Above 22.5	98	18	A
21.50	97	17	B
20.50	96	16	C
19.50	95	15	D
18.50	94	14	E
–	Outside slightly stained	11	Fair cocoon
–	–	8	Ungradable

Kumar *et al.* (2013) developed software to compute various calculations required at different stages in sericulture for the evaluation and proper development of the industry in right direction by harvesting stable cocoon crop with better qualitative and quantitative characters. They stated that by putting the value of shell ration and defective cocoon per cent in the developed software, the value of renditta by non-destructive method can be estimated. Further, the market value of cocoon can be assessed by dividing the raw silk price (which can be obtained through internet via silk exchange) by renditta as furnished below –

Shell Ratio: 18.0

↓

Defective cocoon %: 5

↓

Raw Silk Price: Rs. 2405/-

↓

Get Renditta: 10.6 (Result)

↓

Cocoon Price per Kg: Rs. 226.88

Need of the hour is to sustain the efforts to organise cocoon markets in time, preferably within the vicinity of rearing belts or district Headquarters for the convenience of the rearers. This will minimize the transportation cost to the rearers and hence improve the returns from the activity which deserves all attention and support.

Bibliography

Ayuzawa, C. I.; Sekido, K.; Yamakawa, U.; Sakurai, W.; Kurata, Y.; Yaginuma, Y. and Tolkoro, Y. (1972), *Handbook of Silkworm Rearing. Agric. Tech. Manual*. Fuji Publication Co. Tokyo, Japan, pp. 114-135.

Balvenkatsubbaiah, M.; Datta, R. K.; Baig, M.; Nataraju, B. and lyengar, M. N. S. (1994), Efficacy of Bleaching Powder As a Disinfectant against the Pathogens of Silkworm, *Bombyx Mori* L. *Indian J. Seric.*, 33: 23-26.

Baqual, M. F.; Haque Rufali, S. Z.; Malik, G. N.; Khan I. L. and Mir, M. A. (2013), Timely Marketing of Cocoons: A Boon for Sericulture Development. *Indian Silk*, 3 (10 and 11): 13.

Benchamin, K. V. and Jolly, M. S. (1986), Principles of Silkworm Rearing in: *Proceeding of Seminar on Problems and Prospects of Sericulture*. Mahalingum, S. (Ed.) pp. 63-106, Vellore, India.

Benchamin, K. V. (1992), Chawki Silkworm Rearing – An Evaluation. *Indian Silk*, 31: 18-20.

Chandrakanth, K. S.; Srinivasbabu, G. K.; Dandin, S. B.; Mathur, V. B. and Mahadevamurthy, T. S. (2004), Development of Improved Mountages. *Indian Silk*, 43: 7-12.

Chen, F.; David, P. and Vollrath. F. (2012), Structure and Physical Properties of Silkworm Cocoons. *Journal of Royal Society Interface*, pp. 1-10.

Dandin, S. B.; Basavaraja, H. K. and Suresh Kumar, N. (2005), *Silkworm Breeds and Hybrids at Galore*. Published by Central Sericultural Research and Training Institute, Mysore, India, pp. 1-51.

Dandin, S. B.; Jayaswal, J. and Giridhar, K. (2000), *Handbook of Sericulture Technologies*. Published by Central Silk Board, Bangalore, India.

Dandin, S. B.; Srinivasbabu, G. K.; Chandrakanth, K. S. and Mathur, V. B. (2005), New Modified Card Board Mountages for Quality Cocoon Production. *The 20th Congress of Sericulture Commission*, France, 229-233.

Das, S. K. and Sengupta, K. (1991), Proper Incubation of Eggs Ensures Proper Hatching and Successful Cocoon Crop. *Indian Silk*, 29: 28-29.

Datta, R. K. and Nanavaty, M. (2007), *Global Silk Industry – A Complete Source Book*. APH Publishing Corporation, New Delhi, pp. 347.

Govindan, R.; Narayanaswamy, T. K. and Magdum, S. B. (1988), Relative Moisture Loss from Leaves of Some Mulberry Varieties During Storage. *Current Res.*, 17(11): 151-153.

Harikrishna, R. and Reddy, D. N. R. (1997), Role of Ants in Sericulture and their Management. *Mysore J. Agric. Sci.*, 31: 185-192.

Harishchandra, M.; Mahendra, P. S. and Mishra, P. N. (1999), Storage of Cocoons and Silk. *Indian Silk*, 37(10): 24-28.

Hinton, H. E. (1981), *Biology of Insect Eggs*. Vol. I, pp. 413, Pregamon Press, Oxford.

Huang, G. R. (1983), Influence of Relative Humidity and Air Currents in the Mounting Room on the Cocoon Quality of *Bombyx Mori* in China. *Canye Kexue*, 9: 90-92.

Kamili, S. and Masoodi, M. A. (2004), *Principles of Temperate Sericulture*. Kalyani, New Delhi, India.

Kataoka, H.; Yuhara, Y.; Tanaka, S. and Sawai, M. (1973), The Sex Separation at Pupal Stage of Silkworm by Means of an Electric Capacity Measurement. *J. Seric. Sci. Japan*, 42: 454-462.

Kawaguchi, Y.; Xu, M.K.; Banno, Y.; Kawarabata, T. and Doira, H. (1996), Egg Shell Architecture in the Wild Silk Moth, *Bombyx Mandarina* Inhibiting China. *Sericologia*, 36(4); 609-618.

Kawakami K. (1999), *Standard New Practical for Commercial Bivoltine Rearing*. PPPBST Project, JICA. Published by Central Sericultural Research and Training Institute, Mysore, India.

Kawakami K. (2002), *Illustrated Working Process of New Bivoltine Silkworm Rearing Technology*. PPPBST Project, JICA. Published by Central Sericultural Research and Training Institute, Mysore, India.

Khan, M. A.; Bhat, M. M. and Singh, T. (2011), *Silkworm Crop Protection – Concepts and Approaches*. Daya Publishing House, New Delhi, India, pp. 224.

Kotoku, K. (1993), On the Mounting for Saving Labour by the Improved Rotary Cocooning Frame in the Silkworm, *Bombyx Mori. Res. Rep. Ehimeken, Seric. Expt. Stn.*, 14: 34-38.

Krishnaswamy, S. (1986), *Appropriate Rearing Technology*. Published by Central Silk Board, Bangalore, India.

Krishnaswamy, S. (1993), *A Practical Guide to Mulberry Silk Cocoon Production in Tropics*. Published by Central Silk Board, Bangalore, India.

Krishnaswamy, S.; Narasirnhanna, M. N.; Suryanarayan, S. R. and Kumararaj, S. (1973), *Sericulture Manual - 2. Silkworm Rearing*, FAO, Agricultural Services Bulletin, 15/3, Rome, Italy.

Kumaresan, P.; Vijaya Prakash, N. B. and Rajan, R. K. (1999), An Economic Evaluation of Different Methods of Silkworm Rearing. *Productivity*, 40: 139-141.

Kumar, P; Srivastava, V. B.; Khare, R.; Singh, P. K. and Sahaf, K. A. (2013), Seri Tool: Useful Software in Sericulture. *Indian Silk*, 3(12): 12-15.

Manishankar, G.; Ujjal, M. and Aniruddha, M. (2008), Effect of Environmental Factors (Temperature and Humidity) on Spinning Worms of Silkworm (*Bombyx Mori* L.). *Research Journal of Chemistry and Environment*, 12(4): 12-18.

Margaritis, L. H. (1985), Structure and Physiology of Eggshell; in *Comprehensive Insect Physiology, Biochemistry and Pharmacology*. Kerkut, G. A. and Gilbert, L. I. (Eds.), Vol. I. pp. 153-230, Pergamon Press, Oxford.

Mathur, S. K. and Singh, T. (1990), Abnormal Eclosion in Silkworm, *Bombyx Mori*. *Indian Text. J.*, 100: 150-151.

Mathur, V. B. and Qadri, S. M. H. (2010), *A Manual on Mountages, Mounting and Harvesting Technology for Quality Cocoon Production*. Published by Central Sericultural Research and Training Institute, Mysore, India.

Mathur, V. B.; Singh, G. P. and Kamble, C. K. (1995), Effect of Photoperiod on the Rearing and Diapause in the Silkworm, *Bombyx Mori* L. *J. Seric.*, 3: 46-49.

Ming, W. S. (1994), *Silkworm Egg Production*. Vol. III., Food and Agriculture Organization, Agricultural Services Bulletin, United Nations, Oxford and IBH Publishing Co. Pvt. Ltd., New Delhi, India.

Mishra, S. N. (1989), Cocoon Deflossing Efficiency of Different Deflossing Systems. *Indian Silk*, 27(9): 34-41.

Miya, K. (1984), Early Embryogenesis of *Bombyx Mori*; in *Insect Ultrastructure*. King, R. C. and Akai, H. (Eds.), Vol. II., pp. 49-72, Plenum Press, New York.

Narayanaswamy, K. C. and Devaiah, M. C. (1999), An Overview on Silkworm Uzi Fly; in *Advances in Mulberry Sericulture*. Devaiah, M. C.; Narayanaswamy, K. C. and Maribashetty, V. G. (eds.), CVG Publications, Bangalore, pp. 475-497.

Pallavi, S. N. and Kamble, C. K. (1997), Disinfections and Hygiene in Sericulture – A Review. *Sericologia*, 37: 401-415.

Patil, C. M. and Gowda, B. L. V. (1986), Environmental Adjustment in Sericulture. *Indian Silk*, 25: 11-14.

Pandey, P.; Tripathi, S. P. and Srivastav, B. M. S. (2006), Effect of Ecological Factors on Larval Duration of Silkworm (*Bombyx Mori* L.). *Journal of Ecophysiology and Occupational Health*, 6: 3-5.

Porter, D. and Vollrath, F. (2009), Silk As A Biomimetic Ideal for Structural Polymers. *Adv. Mater.*, 21: 487-492.

Rahmathulla, V. K. (1999), Management of Climatic Factors during Silkworm Rearing. *The Textile Industry and Trade Journal*, pp. 25-26.

Rahmathulla, V. K. (2012), Management of Climatic Factors for Successful (*Bombyx Mori* L.) Crop and Higher Silk Production – A Review. *Psyche*, 1-12.

Rahmathulla, V. K.; Tilakraj, S. and Rajan, R. K. (2006), Influence of Moisture Content in Mulberry Leaf on Growth and Silk Production in *Bombyx Mori. Caspian Journal of Environmental Sciences*, 4(1): 25-30.

Rajan, R. K. and Himantharaj, M. T. (2005), *A Text Book on Silkworm Rearing Technology*. Published by Central Silk Board, Bangalore, India.

Rajan, R. K.; Muroga, A. and Datta, R. K. (1996), *A Manual on Young Silkworm Rearing*. Published by BSTD Project, JICA, Central Sericultural Research and Training Institute, Mysore, India, pp. 1-24.

Rajan, R. K.; Muroga, A. and Datta, R. K. (1997), *A Manual on Mounting and Harvesting Technologies*. Published by BSTD Project, JICA, Central Sericultural Research and Training Institute, Mysore, India, pp. 1-24.

Ramachandra, Y. I.; Bali, G. and Padmalatha Rai, S. (2001), Effect of Temperature and Relative Humidity on Spinning Behaviour of Silkworm (*Bombyx Mori* L.). *Indian Journal of Experimental Biology*, 39(1): 87-89.

Rao Vijayalakshmi; Reddy, V. G.; Jingade, H. A. and Samson, M. V. (1998), Silkworm Egg Incubation. *Indian Textile Journal*, 109(1): 32-37.

Rapusas, H. R. and Gabriel, B. P. (1976), Suitable Temperature, Humidity and Larval Density in the Rearing of *Bombyx Mori. Phillipp. Agric.*, 60: 130-138.

Reddy, D. N. R.; Kotikal, Y. K.; Vijayendra, M. and Subbarayudu. B.V. (1989), Rat Menace and Its Management in Sericulture. *Indian Silk*, 28(2): 53-55.

Reddy, D. N. R.; Vijayendra, M. and Narayanaswamy, K. C. (1995), Studies on the Ants Associated with Sericulture Rearing Houses and Grainages. *Indian J. Ecol.*, 22: 109-112.

Reddy, V.; Rao, V. and Kamble, C. K. (2005), *Manual on Silkworm Eggs, Bombyx Mori*. Published by Silkworm Seed Technology Laboratory, Central Silk Board, Bangalore, India.

Roychoudhury, N.; Paul, D. C. and Subba Rao, G. (1991), Growth, Fecundity and Hatchability of Eggs of *Bombyx Mori* in Relation to Rearing Space. *Entomon*, 16: 203-207.

Samson, M. V.; Chandrashekharaiah and Singh, T. (1994), Seri-post Cocoons Transcription and Deflossing. *Indian Textile Journal*, January, pp. 22-26.

Sekharappa, B. M.; Gururaj, C. S.; Raghuraman, K. and Dandin, S. B. (1993), *Shoot Rearing for Late Age Silkworms*. Published by KSSRDI, Thalghatapura, Bangalore, India.

Sengupta, K.; Singh, B. D. and Mustafa, R. (1971), A Study on the Effect of Time of Harvest of Mulberry Leaf on Silkworm Cocoon Crop and Quality. *Indian J. Seric.*, 10: 1-5.

Sharma, A. K. (1992), Economic Characters of Mulberry Silkworm (*Bombyx Mori*) in Relation to the Rearing Methods. *Biol. Mem.*, 18: 19-22.

Shivakumaraswamy, M. P.; Bhaskar, R. N.; Chandraprakash, J. and Sudharshana, I. (2004) Influence of Method of Mulberry Leaf Preservation on Rearing Performance of Silkworm, *Bombyx Mori* L. *Bull. Ind. Acad. Seric.*, 8(1): 55-60.

Singh, R.; Kalpana, G. B.; Sudhaker Rao, P. and Ahsan, M. M. (1998), Studies on Cocoon Shapes in Different Crosses of the Mulberry Silkworm, Bombyx mori L. *Indian Journal of Sericulture*, 37(1): 85-88.

Singh, T. (2001), Influence of Rearing Space on Economic Traits in the Silkworm, *Bombyx Mori* L. *Bull. Ind. Acad. Seri.*, 5: 111-113.

Singh, T. and Saratchandra, B. (2004), *Principles and Techniques of Silkworm Seed Production*. Discovery Publishing House, New Delhi, pp. 359.

Singh, T.; Bhat, M. M. and Khan, M. A. (2010), *Silkworm Egg Science – Principles and Protocols*. Daya Publishing House, New Delhi, pp. 278.

Singh, T.; Vijayalakshmi Rao; Jingade, A. H. and Samson, M. V. (2002), Structure and Development of Silkworm Eggs. *Sericologia* (France), 43(3): 323-334.

Takami, T. (1946), Experimental Studies on the Embryo Formation in *Bombyx Mori*. V. Presumptive Mesodermal and Neural Regions of the Eggs. *Seibutu*, 1: 208-211.

Tazima, Y. (1964), *The Genetics of the Silkworm*. Logos Press, London.

Tazima, Y. (1978), *Silkworm Egg*. Published by Central Silk Board, Bangalore, India.

Thiagarajan, V. and Govindaiah (1987), Menace of Dermestid Beetles in Grainages. *Indian Silk*, 26: 26-27.

Ullal, S. R. and Narasimhanna, M. N. (1994), *Handbook of Practical Sericulture*. Published by Central Silk Board, Bangalore, India.

Vijayaveer, Negi, B. K. and Rao, K. M. (1996), Dermestic Beetles and Some Insect Pests Associated with Stored Silkworm Cocoons in India, Including a World List of Dermestid Species Found Attacking this Commodity. *J. Stored Proc. Res.*, 32: 69-89.

Vijayakumari, K. M.; Balavenkatasubbiah, B.; Rajan, R. K.; Himantharaj, H. T.; Nataraj, B. and Rekha, B. (2001) Influence of Temperature and Relative Humidity on the Rearing Performance and Disease Incidence in CSR Hybrid Silkworm, *Bombyx Mori* L. *International Journal of Industrial Entomology*, 3(2): 113-116.

Wu, P. C. and Chen, D. C. (1992), *Silkworm Rearing*. FAO, Agricultural Services Bulletin, Rome, Italy.

Yamashita, O. and Hasegawa, K. (1985), Embryonic Diapause; in *Comprehensive Insect Physiology, Biochemistry and Pharmacology*. Kerkut, G. A. and Gilbert, L. I. (Eds.), Vol. I., pp. 407-434, Pergamon Press, Oxford.

Index

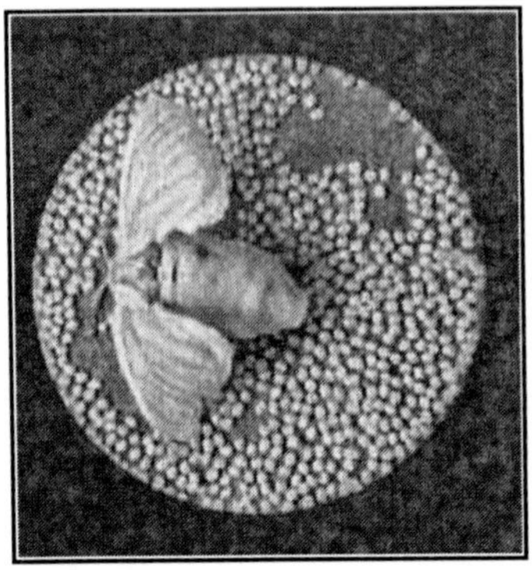

Freshly Laid Silkworm Egg

Grown Silkworm Larva

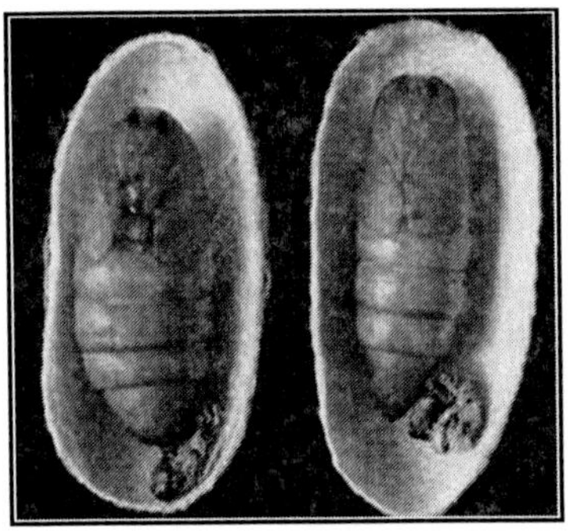

Female and Male
Silkworm Pupa

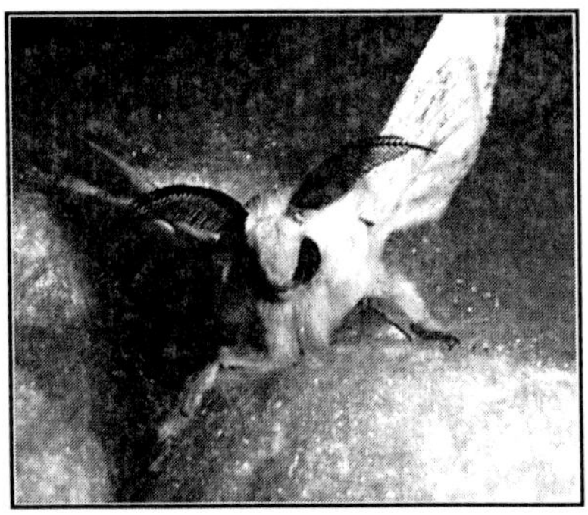

Adult Silkworm Moth

White and Yellow Coloured Cocoon

V I Mulberry Variety
(Good Quality Leaf)

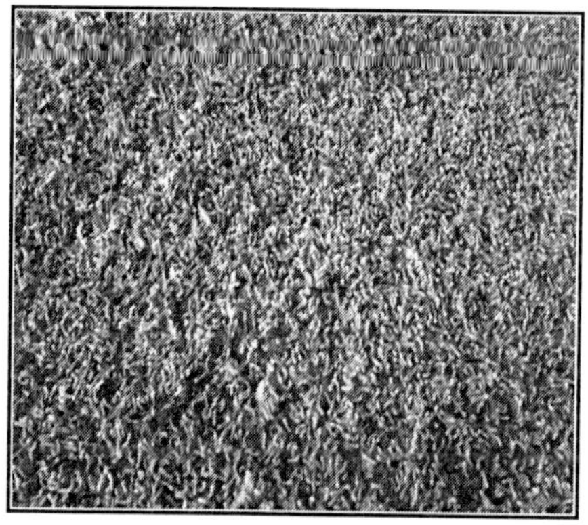

Newly Hatched
Silkworm Larvae

Chopping of Mulberry Leaf

Chawki Leaf (S146
Mulberry Variety

Dusting of Bed Disifectant

Rearing Trays, Rearing Stand
and Loose Egg Boxes

Rearing by Farmer on Rearing Racks

Health 4th Stage Larvae Feeding on Mulberry Leaves

Silkworm Larvae in 4th Moult

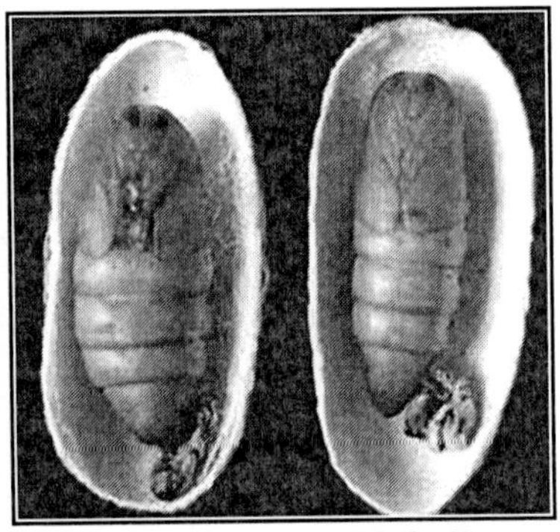

Female Pupa Male Pupa

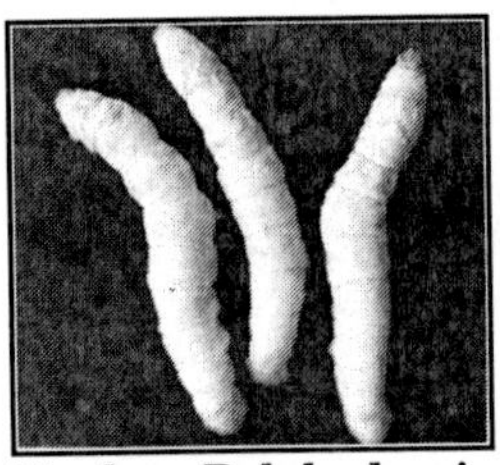

Nuclear Polyhedrosis

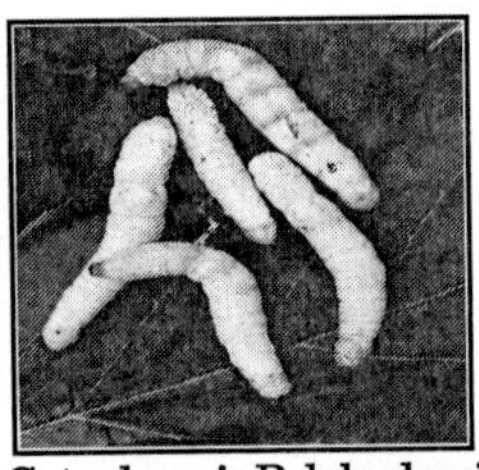

Cytoplasmic Polyhedrosis

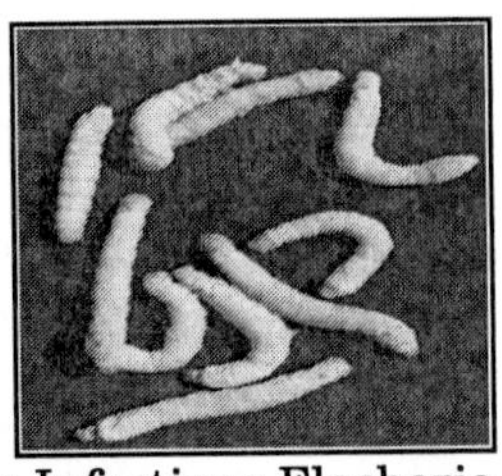

Infectious Flacherie

Densonucleosis

Black Thorax Septicemia

Sotto Disease

White Muscardine

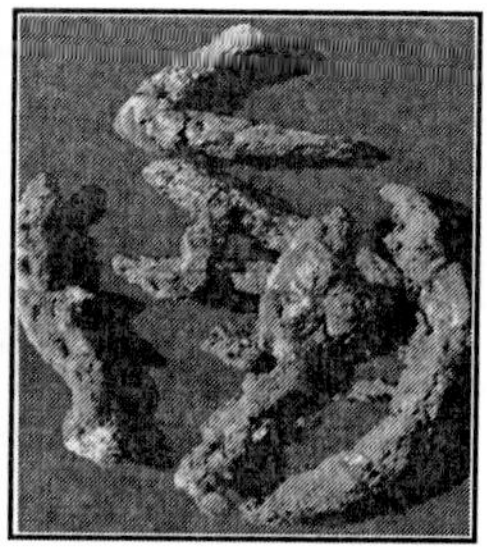

Green Muscardine

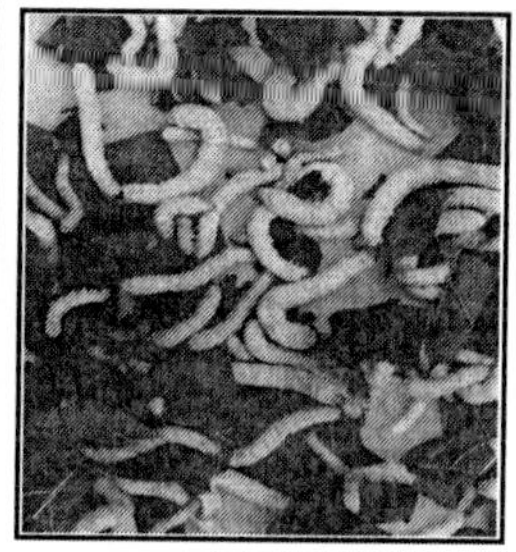

Perbrine Affected Larvae

Mature Larvae Spinning Cocoon on Plastic Mountage

Collapsible Plastic Mountage with Cocoon

Bivoltine Cocoon with Floss

Silkworm Cocoons Damaged by Dermestid Beetle